G. H. Mead

G. H. Mead

A Critical Introduction

Filipe Carreira da Silva

polity

First published in 2007 by Polity Press

Polity Press
65 Bridge Street
Cambridge CB2 1UR, UK

Polity Press
350 Main Street
Malden, MA 02148, USA

ISBN-13: 978-07456-3457-9
ISBN-13: 978-07456-3458-6 (pb)

A catalogue record for this book is available from the British Library.

Typeset in 10 on 11.5 pt Palatino
by SNP Best-set Typesetter Ltd, Hong Kong
Printed and bound in India by Replika Press PVT Ltd, Kundli

The publisher has used its best endeavours to ensure that the URLs for external websites referred to in this book are correct and active at the time of going to press. However, the publisher has no responsibility for the websites and can make no guarantee that a site will remain live or that the content is or will remain appropriate.

Every effort has been made to trace all copyright holders, but if any have been inadvertently overlooked the publishers will be pleased to include any necessary credits in any subsequent reprint or edition.

For further information on Polity, visit our website: www.polity.co.uk

Contents

Acknowledgements

This book has been almost two years in the making, and during that time I have inevitably incurred more debts of gratitude than I could hope to acknowledge here. I would like to begin by expressing my indebtedness to Emma Longstaff, my editor at Polity, for many important suggestions and invaluable advice, as well as for her consistent interest in the project. To Sue Birley, who has proofread my work and checked my English since my PhD days, I owe my sincerest thanks. I would also like to mention Teresa Sousa Fernandes, whose intellectual generosity is a shining example to all those who are lucky enough to cross her path. I owe special appreciation to Mónica Brito Vieira, a model of how academic and personal excellence can meet; our discussions of assorted arguments have gone on for several years now. Most of all, however, I thank Sofia Aboim, whose unrivalled support and forbearance, especially throughout the last stages of the manuscript, will never be fully repaid; and my family – Beatriz, Lourdes, Leila, and most especially my father, to whom this book is dedicated. Finally it remains to thank my friends and staff in Wolfson College, Cambridge, for all their affection during the summers of 2005 and 2006.

1

Introduction and General Overview

A century has passed since George Herbert Mead (1863–1931) started working on the social theory that would grant him a place in the socio-logical canon, and yet his writings have lost none of their appeal. The reason why Mead's ideas are after all these years still so engaging is, I argue, that the last two *fins de siècle* share certain structural similarities. Very much as in Mead's time, Western modernity is experiencing today a sense of profound crisis, which follows a relatively long period of confidence in the rational mastery of social problems. In such epochs of crisis, the best theoretical instruments are those able to deal with change, uncertainty and hybridism. From this perspective, I think we have a lot to learn from Mead, perhaps the sociological classic who (with Simmel) best responded to the conceptual challenges posed by the first crisis of Western modernity. Rejecting the pessimism one can find in other classics' writings (just recall Weber's theses on bureauc-ratization or on the disenchantment of the modern world), Mead was confident that science and democracy could be reconciled in the form of a naturalistic and evolutionary social science, which conceives of the human mind as an 'emergent' from – that is, an entity resulting from – symbolic interaction.

Among the sociological classics, Mead occupies a special position. Although he lived in the same epoch as all the other 'founding fathers' of sociology (he was five years younger than Durkheim and one year older than Weber), he is not only one of the few to have exerted a pro-found and lasting influence on a discipline other than his own, but also the only American to figure in that canonical gallery. In fact, Mead was not a sociologist; he was, by training, a philosopher with a strong interest in social psychology. The brilliance of his ideas on the social nature of the human self, however, ensured that in disciplines such as sociology and social psychology Mead is still seen today as one of the predecessors of their greatest practitioners. Unlike Marx, Weber or Durkheim, Mead was not a prolific writer. It was in the classroom, thinking aloud in the silent presence of his students, that Mead was at his best. This personal preference for the spoken word is very much in accord with the always 'in-the-making' nature of his intellectual edifice. Far from being a rigid, all-encompassing philosophical system, Mead's thinking is best described as a system in a state of flux.

Western modernity, the self, the scientific method and democratic politics are the conceptual reference points to which Mead returned time and time again, from his early short paper on 'The Working Hypothesis on Social Reform' (1899) or the important but neglected 'The Definition of the Psychical' (1903) to his last written work, the 1930 Carus Lectures, published posthumously in *The Philosophy of the Present* (1932). Like many others of his generation, Mead crossed the Atlantic to study in Germany, the most reputed academic milieu of the epoch. After a brief period at Ann Arbor, he was eventually offered a position at the University of Chicago, where he arrived in 1894 and would remain until the end of his career. In several ways, Mead was in the right place at the right time. At the turn of the century, the city of Chicago was a great laboratory of social experiences, ranging from large-scale processes of urbanization, industrialization and migration to many other pressing social issues on a smaller scale. Intellectually speaking, Mead could not have wished for a better place to be in than the University of Chicago – this was at the time when the famous 'Chicago school' of sociology was created by his colleagues from the sociology department, just a few doors down the corridor. In more general terms, Mead lived in an age of rapid change and growing uncertainty, an epoch of great optimism regarding the possibilities of human reason, yet one of profound distrust concerning the naive positivistic belief in progress. Such an intellectual atmosphere proved to be the perfect environment in which to develop a theoretical solution for a problem that has haunted social thinkers since the dawn of the Western variant of modernity – how to reconcile the seemingly intractable tension between an ever more individualistic self and an increasingly universalistic social order. Mead's answer to this question, which will be discussed in detail later, still ranks today among the most valuable elements of what could be called 'the heritage of sociology'.[1]

Mead's confessed difficulties in putting his thoughts into writing also helps to explain why several generations of social scientists were introduced to his ideas through *Mind, Self, and Society*, an anthology of transcripts of his lectures on social psychology. Although this book does provide an enjoyable and accessible entrée to Mead's ideas, its editorial quality is questionable and creates an excessively partial image of Mead's contributions. Of course, one can avoid these difficulties by reading other books by Mead,[2] as well as the best available secondary literature (I am thinking about the books by Joas and Cook, whose merits will be discussed later), even though in this case the non-specialist reader might find them too difficult and overly focused on Mead's intellectual biography. While writing the present book I kept this double challenge in mind. I have thus tried to write a critical introduction to Mead's ideas that is accessible enough for students and the general public, but which is at the same time able to provide food for thought for professional social scientists. I would suggest to the first category that they pay particular attention to chapters 3 to 5, where I discuss Mead's social psychology in detail; to those already acquainted with Mead's ideas, I hope the last portion of the book makes a contribution to current debates on the condition of our age, as it clarifies Mead's contributions to the resolution of the conceptual challenges we currently face.

There are several notions that social practitioners have become accustomed to associate with Mead – the gesture and the significant symbol, the I–me distinction and the 'generalized other', or the concept of 'taking the role of the other' – but to my mind none encapsulates better the very rationale of his communicative social theory than the idea of dialogue. From thinking, conceived by Mead as a sort of 'inner conversation', to the resolution of international conflicts, Mead consistently favoured a dialogical perspective. Of course, this is not to say that he gave every research area the same degree of attention. As I will show, Mead's version of intersubjectivism is especially developed as far as the inner structure of the human self is concerned – Mead's account of the social and communicative nature of the self is rightly considered to be his chief contribution to today's social sciences. Along with figures such as John Dewey, Martin Buber, Mikhail Bakhtin, Hans-Georg Gadamer, Jürgen Habermas and Richard Rorty, Mead produced one of the most important dialogical social theories of the twentieth century.

A summary of Mead's ideas

A substantial part of this book (chapters 2 to 5) will be spent clarifying and detailing the ideas that make up Mead's system of thinking. The first of Mead's key ideas is the notion of 'taking the role of the other'. However, unlike authors like Erving Goffman (whose dramaturgical approach, developed in seminal works such as *The Presentation of Self in Everyday Life* [1959], is one of the most sophisticated models to be developed within the symbolic interactionist paradigm), Mead does not wish to explore the theatrical dimensions of this concept. For this reason, I will use 'role' and 'attitude' interchangeably. By 'taking the attitude of the other' Mead wishes to convey the idea that individuals are able to import into their conduct a *behavioural disposition* to respond in a similar way to other individuals responding to a given type of stimulus. Consider the example Mead chooses to explain this notion to his students: when a child plays with a friend, he 'is calling out in him the corresponding activities of the other person involved';[3] the attitude that the child imports into his conduct, say, paying out money, is also the response that this attitude calls out in the other: the child is stimulated by the response he is calling out in his friend. Although this example refers to the simplest form of role-taking, it is not difficult to grasp some of the functions it performs in Mead's social psychology. Two of these functions should be emphasized at this point. Firstly, the concept of 'taking the role of the other' helps Mead to explain thinking as a kind of 'inner conversation': by importing the attitudes of others into their conduct, individuals acquire the ability to see the world from the perspective of these others; this sort of reflective intelligence is exactly what distinguishes human thinking. Moreover, since such a reflective intelligence emerges 'through the internalization by the individual of social processes of experience and behavior',[4] that is, through adopting the attitude of other individuals, Mead finds himself in a position from which he can conceive of thinking as a social process. Secondly, and related to the next key idea I wish to present, the concept of 'taking the role of the other' helps Mead to clarify the behavioural origins of 'significant symbols'. It is this particular behavioural mechanism, he argues, that allows the emergence of the consciousness of meaning. In order to understand the implications of the concept of 'taking the role of the other', let us now turn to the next central element of Mead's social psychology, namely the notions of meaning and of the significant symbol.

In brief, what is at stake here is the transformation of a vocal gesture (a sound) into an element of a natural language (a word). Vocal gestures become significant or meaningful, Mead argues, only in the context of a social interaction. In particular, a significant symbol emerges when its carrier provokes, both in the individual uttering it and in the individual listening to it, a stimulus that is simultaneously a response. What does Mead mean by this? Imagine two friends saying farewell at an airport. One of them makes a gesture (let us say he waves), which elicits in the other individual a certain response (she waves back at him). By responding to the gesture of the first individual, the second interprets that gesture – her response brings out the meaning of his gesture. For Mead, the meaning of an object – say, a gesture – is not something intrinsic to it (its 'essence'); rather, it is an emergent of social interaction – it is an objective element in the behavioural structure that connects organisms to the surrounding environment.

A third central idea put forth by Mead refers to his conception of the structure of the self. Very much as in the case of the previous two ideas,

Mead favours here a socially constituted and objectively defined notion. The fact that in this case the notion in question is the very one most closely associated with subjectivity only reaffirms the naturalistic and experimental character of Mead's 'scientific social psychology'. It is also, and fundamentally, a processual view of reality that is espoused by Mead (as opposed to a Cartesian, mechanistic and rationalistic one). There are two main components to Mead's treatment of the self.

On the one hand, Mead discusses it from the perspective of childhood development. In particular, the genesis of the self is explained by means of two developmental stages. The first is the stage of 'play', during which children learn how to put themselves in the place of another individual: it is at this time that children acquire a self – they do that by learning to take the role of other individuals. The second developmental stage is that of 'game', a more elaborate and demanding social experience. Here children have to take the role not only of a single individual, but of all the individuals involved in the game; moreover, children have to learn how to coordinate their actions according to the rules of the game. Only at this stage do children acquire a fully developed self. The generalized character specific to adult selves is thus the outcome of a two-step developmental process, the success of which depends on the nature of the social experiences we are all exposed to during our childhood. At this juncture, Mead introduces one of his best-known concepts, the notion of the 'generalized other'. Through this notion he wishes to convey the idea of an internalized set of social attitudes: by learning how to take the role of the 'generalized other', children acquire the ability to import the attitudes of the social group into their own selves. They thus begin to see themselves from the perspective of everyone else. One of Mead's favoured examples to explain the 'generalized other' is the baseball game. Each player has to incorporate, besides the rules of the game, the perspectives of everyone else into her own performance: she has to see the game as everyone else sees it. Only in this way will she be able to play baseball, or any other collective game or activity, for that matter – and this is Mead's point exactly. Cooperative activities such as games are, so to speak, the prelude to social life. By learning how to take the attitude of the 'generalized other' while playing baseball children gradually acquire a socio-psychological ability of central importance. This said, it is not difficult to see why Mead grants so crucial an importance to educational matters (even if it is in Dewey rather than Mead that we find the most elaborate classical pragmatist statement on education).

On the other hand, Mead analyses the self from the viewpoint of its internal structure. Following the insights of his fellow pragmatists William James and John Dewey, he conceives of the self as an ongoing social process with two distinct phases: the 'I', which is described as the spontaneous response of the individual to the social situation, and the 'me', a socially structured, conscious self-image that we build by seeing ourselves through the eyes of the others. The I–me distinction can best be understood by reference to the memory image we have of ourselves. Imagine yourself having breakfast this morning: you can see yourself having milk and cereals, talking to your parents and so on. What I wish to emphasize is the distinction between you, now in the present, remembering yourself this morning having breakfast, and your remembered self-image, located in the past. Mead calls these two aspects (or facets) of the self the 'I' and the 'me' – the 'I' is that phase of the self that remembers while the 'me' is the remembered self-image. As we shall see, from this very simple and intuitive beginning, Mead developed a sophisticated account of the inner workings of the human mind. In short, for Mead, the 'I' is a source of novelty and creativity, indispensable for the assertion of individuality, while the 'me' refers to the set of organized social attitudes within one's self. The rigid distinction between inner, subjective life and external, objective reality is thus ruled out by Mead; on the contrary, he conceives of the self as a process through which social experiences are permanently being incorporated into the self (through the 'me') and reconstructed by the 'I'. Selves are thus natural, evolving social products.

Mead's vision of the relation between the individual and society makes it thoroughly naturalistic, evolutionary (though not to be confused with social Darwinism) and cooperative. It also makes it, and fundamentally, a process. The 'I' and the 'me' are but phases of a larger process, the self, which in turn is but a phase of an even larger process, society. Each phase can only be fully understood by reference not only to the process in which it is located, but also to the larger process in which the former takes place: general changes in societal values and norms can thus be seen to influence transformations at the level of individual consciousness and vice versa. This is why Mead sees religious or intellectual geniuses, such as Jesus or Socrates, as individuals whose 'Is' were exceptionally innovative and powerful: the course of history can be profoundly changed by the least probable element, the unconscious and unpredictable 'I'.

Standing on the shoulders of giants

These are the contributions that earned Mead his place in the sociological canon. Of course, to paraphrase Newton, Mead is able to see further only because he is standing on the shoulders of giants. In what follows, I examine the sources from which Mead draws throughout his career. His originality and current relevance are, I argue, better appreciated against the backdrop of the figures that most directly influenced his thought. In fact, Mead's intellectual context can offer an unparalleled opportunity to grasp the logical structure of his social and political thinking. By reconstructing the dialogues in which Mead engages throughout his career I wish to do justice to the dialogical nature of his system of thought. The engagements between Mead and Immanuel Kant, Georg Wilhelm Friedrich Hegel, Charles Darwin, Josiah Royce, John Dewey, William James, Wilhelm Wundt, John B. Watson, Henri Bergson and Alfred North Whitehead can enlighten an important aspect of Mead's theoretical strategy, namely the appropriation of other authors' concepts and theories according to his own agenda and interests. Again, the relevant context is not necessarily the most immediate one. As such, some of the dialogues in which Mead can be said to have taken part are with authors who are not his contemporaries.

Kant and Hegel are two examples of authors from a different era with whom Mead engages in dialogue on several occasions. I would like to call my readers' attention to the fact that this particular dialogue does not make easy reading, especially for an undergraduate audience. It is, however, of crucial importance to understand the extent to which German idealism, in particular the writings of Kant and Hegel, is one of the most enduring philosophical influences over Mead's thinking. To begin with, Mead's (never completed) doctoral dissertation revolved around the empiricist conception of space, which was supposed to be criticized with the aid of Kant. Mead, however, intended to go beyond Kant with the aid of physiological psychology: space would thus not be seen, as suggested by Kant, as a form of intuition but as the product of the cooperation between eye and hand. I will return to this important issue in my discussion of Mead's intellectual biography. Of course, Kant's influence over Mead extends well beyond the latter's doctoral project. Indeed, Kant's influence can be detected in all the authors who came to be associated with pragmatism. From the adaptation of Kant's theories by Peirce, there emerged the distinctively pragmatist 'treatment of the cognitive subject by reference to the concepts of experience, habits, novelty, language, community, inquiry and evolution'.[5] This can be seen throughout Mead's career: from Kantian ethics to his transcendental logic, there are numerous instances where one can see Mead, time and again, critically engaging 'the philosopher of the revolution', the title Mead used to qualify Kant in his 1928 lectures *Movements of Thought in the Nineteenth Century*. Mead's engagement with Kant's moral philosophy is of particular relevance. Regarding Kant's categorical imperative – 'Act only according to that maxim by which you can at the same time will that it would become a universal law' – Mead subscribes to its universalist character but criticizes its inadequacy to deal with the resolution of concrete moral problems. Mead's alternative points to the need for a creative moral reconstruction, in which the moral agent must take into account all of the relevant conflicting interests. In other words, while retaining Kant's orientation to universalism,

Mead rejects Kant's transcendental subject in favour of a concrete communicative community.

Let us now turn to Hegel. From several of Mead's early philosophical writings down to his aforementioned lectures on *Movements of
Thought in the Nineteenth Century*, where Hegel is shown as a precursor
to evolutionist theories whose dialectical method was at odds with the
experimental method favoured by science,[6] Hegel can certainly be said
to be a privileged interlocutor who helped in shaping Mead's intellectual position. This holds true especially for some of Mead's earliest
book reviews, where he explicitly asserted his indebtedness to Hegel.
Both in the attempt by Gustav Class to combine Hegel's 'objective
spirit' and Schleiermacher's 'personal individuality'[7] and in Charles
D'Arcy's proposal to reconcile Hegel and Berkeley,[8] Mead emphasizes
the same point. Hegel's dialectic method, responsible for transforming
philosophy into a 'method of thought rather than a search for fundamental entities',[9] constitutes the method 'by which the self in its full
cognitive and social content meets and solves its difficulties',[10] i.e. it
reveals the fundamental continuity between the 'method of intelligence' and human consciousness itself. This said, however, the evolution of Mead's system of thought explains how, from this almost
enthusiastic endorsement of Hegel's philosophy in the 1890s and early
1900s, he came in the 1920s to adopt an increasingly critical position
on Hegel's dialectic method.

The evolutionary framework in which Mead is operating derives
from Darwin's theory of the origin of the species. By putting Hegel
in dialogue with Darwin, Mead is able to suggest that Hegel's 'philosophy of evolution' is a speculative precursor to Darwin's scientific
breakthrough, and one which enabled philosophy to overcome the
dichotomy between mechanistic and teleological theories of evolution.
From his conversation with Darwin, Mead took the naturalistic outlook
that would accompany him during the rest of his career.

One can now glimpse at the truly dialogical nature of Mead's system
of thought. In making Hegel join in his conversations with Royce and
Dewey, Mead let himself be introduced to German idealism and to the
functionalist social psychology that he would advocate until the 1910s.
In the debate with Royce (Mead, 1909), Mead was particularly interested in criticizing his theory of the social character of linguistic meaning
and human reflection. While Royce advocated that altruistic other-
consciousness and egoistic self-consciousness were mutually implied
in each other, since one can be conscious of oneself only in relation to
a real or ideal fellow, Mead retorted that

> [s]ocial consciousness is the presupposition of imitation, and when Pro-
> fessor Royce . . . makes imitation the means of getting the meaning of
> what others and we ourselves are doing, he seems to be either putting

the cart before the horse, or else to be saying that the ideas which we have of the actions of the others are ideo-motor in their character, but this does not make out of imitation the means of their becoming ideo-motor.[11]

But it was with Dewey that Mead had the most lasting and significant dialogue. This dialogue, which eventually evolved into a friendship, started under the influence of the writings on psychology of another thinker associated with American pragmatism, William James. Mead met Dewey at the University of Michigan in Ann Arbor, shortly after his return from Germany, at a moment when Dewey was engaged in an active exchange of letters with James concerning the latter's *Principles of Psychology* (1890). The outcome of this exchange of arguments and ideas was, on Dewey's part, the criticism of the social-psychological 'reflex arc' model and the development of the alternative 'organic circuit' conception of action, according to which human thinking proceeds by solving problems in specific contexts.[12] The voice of Charles Sanders Peirce can also be heard in this argument; Mead made it his own, in order to engage, again, in a dialogue with Hegel. In 'Suggestions Towards a Theory of the Philosophical Disciplines' (1900), Mead uses Dewey's article on the 'reflex arc' as a foundation for his groundwork on a new logic, understood in the Hegelian sense of a theory of intelligent action.[13] For my purposes, however, the most relevant topic of discussion between Mead and Dewey is their shared conception of radical democracy, in the formation of which the ideological setting of turbulent 1890s Chicago played a significant role. Symptomatically, while debating what would be the best form of democratic government, both Mead and Dewey draw on the scientific ideal of the free exchange of rational arguments, to reach a conception of radical democracy in which rational experimentation and civic participation are different sides of the same coin.

It is around a different topic, though, that the dialogue between Mead, James and Wilhelm Wundt evolves. It is a debate concerning the nature of the object of psychology, in which Mead adopts a critical stance against the so-called mentalistic psychology of consciousness in favour of a notion of consciousness that privileges a functional conception of the psychical.[14] In a consciously dialogical way, Mead starts by convoking all the proponents of competing doctrines of the psychical. Wundt, Külpe, Bradley, Bosanquet, Ward and Stout, James – all are invited to join in the debate on the definition of the psychical. From the exchange with Wundt, Mead learns three things. Firstly, he appropriates Wundt's concept of 'gesture', to supplement his own socio-linguistic explanation of the genesis of the mind. As we will see in detail later on, this notion of gesture plays a pivotal role in Mead's social psychology. Secondly, he comes to the view that a correspondence theory of truth should be rejected in favour of the pragmatist epistemological stance suggested by Dewey. Thirdly, he adopts the position that the solution to overcoming the dualism between body and psyche cannot lie in a double structure of the object of psychology; rather, it can be reached only if subjectivity is submitted to the same kind of analysis as the objective elements of human consciousness. Mead is advocating here the unity of consciousness; but this is precisely what James had achieved through his notion of 'stream of consciousness', 'by all odds the richest statement of the psychical consciousness that philosophic literature has yet presented'.[15]

Yet, having said this, it must be admitted that Mead had some reservations concerning the methodological strategy employed by James. In his view, once an adequate concept of the psychical is defined, we will be able to reconstruct the otherwise useful Jamesian notion of 'stream of consciousness' in order to identify its origins and functions. Indeed, with Mead's definition of the psychical one can see, not only James's distinction between 'I' and 'me' being appropriated for the first time, but also the way Mead tries to respond to the challenges of overcoming the body–psyche dualism, of providing a non-individualist conception of the individual, and of developing a reconstructive definition of individual cognition:

> For this functional psychology an explicit definition of its subject-matter seems highly important. That suggested in this paper is as follows: that phase of experience within which we are immediately conscious of conflicting impulses which rob the object of its character as object-stimulus, leaving us in so far in an attitude of subjectivity; but during which a new object-stimulus appears due to the reconstructive activity which is identified with the subject 'I' as distinct from the object 'me'.[16]

With this definition Mead concluded what can be considered to be his 'most significant work prior to the development of his fundamental premises for a theory of interaction and a social psychology'.[17] At this point, it is instructive to discuss the relationship between Mead and John B. Watson, a former student of his. Due to its strategic character, the Mead–Watson dialogue allows us to address two important issues: the clarification of the nature of Mead's behaviourism in opposition to Watson's proposals and the terminological problems associated with the labelling of Mead's social-psychological thought.

Firstly, by the time Mead published his 'The Definition of the Psychical', behaviourism was far from enjoying a dominant position in American social psychology: it was only in 1913, a decade after the publication of Mead's paper, that Watson published 'Psychology as the Behaviorist Views It', the article that put behaviourism at the centre of the social-psychological agenda. There is thus no factual basis to support the long-held thesis that Mead's strand of behaviourism represents a kind of a retort to Watson's proposals. On the contrary, there are good reasons to suggest that Mead's behaviourism is actually a version completely independent from Watsonian behaviourism. This can be seen, for instance, in the first sections of *Mind, Self, and Society*, where Mead defines his own position by contrasting his views with those espoused by the 'behaviorist of the Watsonian type'.[18] What distinguishes the latter's behaviourism? To begin with, Watson suggests that psychology should focus on human conduct 'as it is observable by others'; this, of course, entails that human consciousness should also be explained in terms of external behaviour. For instance, human thinking, according to Watson, can be studied in terms 'of language symbols: 'these symbols were not necessarily uttered loudly enough to be heard by others, and often only involved the muscles of the throat without leading to audible speech. That was all there was to thought', Mead critically observes.[19]

As we shall see in detail later on, there are good reasons for Mead to criticize the reductionistic character of Watson's strand of behaviourism. It is not merely a question of Mead's behaviourism being more sensitive to non-observable phenomena and to the social context than that of Watson is. Rather, Mead's social psychology is, as Joas rightly puts it, 'an independent conception radically different from Watson's behaviourism'.[20] In fact, as Mead makes abundantly clear, his behaviourism, far from ignoring consciousness, tries to analyse it 'functionally, and as a natural rather than a transcendental phenomenon'.[21] Mead's naturalistic and functionalistic perspective evolves, so to speak, between Scylla and Charybdis: it tries to avoid both introspectionism (as displayed in the Wundtian-inspired study of states of consciousness) and Watsonian behaviourism (which simply rules out the existence of anything like consciousness), treating them as two equally undesirable alternatives. Mead's proposal points, on the one hand, to a study of consciousness no less objective than Watson's behaviourism (if anything, even more so), and, on the other hand, to one that is no less sensitive than Wundtian structuralism to the complexity and subtleness of the issue at hand.

However – and this is the second issue I would like to address – I must once more call my readers' attention to the poor editorial quality of *Mind, Self, and Society*. In this particular case, the implications of Morris' creative editorial work are not trivial. Contrary to what is widely assumed, Mead never refers to his version of behaviourism as 'social behaviourism'; when Mead allegedly says '[o]ur behaviorism is a social behaviorism',[22] one of the two passages in *Mind, Self, and Society* where one can find Mead using this expression is actually an insertion by Morris.[23] To suggest, as Morris does, that Mead's behaviourism is a *social* behaviourism, in contrast to Watsonian behaviourism, seems to indicate that what separates their social-psychological thought is only a question of the degree to which social affairs are taken into consideration. On the contrary, as I have just tried to explain, while Watson's behaviourism subsumes consciousness to the realm of external, observable phenomena, Mead's behaviourism not only accepts the existence of an inner psychic life but proposes to study it as an integral part of the natural world: as such, thought processes (imagination, reflection, etc.) are no less amenable to scientific scrutiny than any other kind of human activity.

It is worth pointing out that the dialogical nature of Mead's theorizing can be traced throughout the entire course of his career, up to the last phase, when Whitehead and Bergson came to be his main intellectual interlocutors. Actually, Mead's engagement with Bergson began in 1907, with the publication of the latter's book *L'Evolution Créatrice*. In opposition to the mechanistic conception of the world, Bergson proposes a conception marked by freedom, novelty and change. In a review of this book, Mead subscribes to Bergson's reservations concerning scientism but rejects the irrationalist implications of his proposal. In the conclusion of that book review, Mead expresses his surprise that Bergson failed to recognize the 'creative power of consciousness in the construction of the very scientific world and its matter which for him stands opposed to thought and life. It seems to be only in the unconscious creations of perceptions and the unreflective phases of voluntary processes that he can perceive the creative fiat which is identical in consciousness and nature'.[24] In the early twenties, Mead returned to Bergson's texts in order to revive this previous encounter and to gather relevant insights for tackling the problem at the centre of his attention at the time: a functional analysis of perception. In the summer of 1927, Mead delivered a course on Bergson's philosophy: a portion of the student notes taken on that occasion was later included in *Movements of Thought in the Nineteenth Century*. In these lectures, one can see Mead restating his earlier criticism that Bergson failed to offer an objective statement of categories such as 'the flow, the freedom, the novelty, the interpenetration, the creativity, upon which he sets such great store', relegating these to the sphere of subjective consciousness.[25] The required correction of Bergson's approach was to be found in Whitehead's philosophy of nature. Human subjectivity can be objectively analysed insofar as its natural character is emphasized. That mind is a natural event is the point upon which Mead wishes to found his scientific social psychology. In fact, while discussing with Whitehead the philosophy of nature and cosmology, Mead invokes Darwin in order to give a natural basis to human sociality. When Mead discusses, in 'The Objective Reality of Perspectives' (1926),[26] the relatedness of two unconnected movements that share the same emphasis on the 'objectivity of perspectives', the naturalistic and developmental logic of his social psychology is combined with the relativist perspective associated with Whitehead.[27] In particular, what Mead wishes to pick out from his dialogue with Whitehead is the latter's 'conception of nature as an organization of perspectives, which are there in nature'.[28]

The dialogical nature of Mead's system of thought emerges from this series of conversations as one of its central features. My goal has been not so much to provide a systematic account of every encounter he experienced during his career as to demonstrate the dialogical character of Mead's theoretical strategy. Drawing on Dewey's remark that Mead's philosophical thinking 'springs from his own intimate experiences, from things deeply felt',[29] one can perhaps go as far as to suggest that Mead actually 'takes the role of the other' every time he engages in a rational exchange of arguments with his interlocutors. To conceive of the mind as an internal 'forum of conversation' is but the logical corollary of Mead's dialogical theoretical strategy.

The structure of the book

As these intellectual engagements show, Mead's chief research interest is the scientific analysis of the origins and development of human consciousness. His was a thoroughly social approach to the problem of the mind – it proceeded, so to speak, from the outside in, not from the inside out. Human subjectivity is thus seen by Mead as a natural, social, evolving process. It emerges out of cooperative social life, through the exchange of linguistic signs. Society first, and then mind and the self: contrary to the order of priority suggested by the title of the book through which generations got to know Mead's ideas, *Mind, Self, and Society*, Mead's social psychology explains the part in terms of the whole, not the whole in terms of its parts. Mead's individuals are social agents as much as they are biological organisms. The naturalism of Mead's social psychology can hardly be overemphasized. But his perspective is naturalistic as much as evolutionary and socially oriented.

At a time of increasing disciplinary specialization such as ours, Mead's work regains relevance. His early groundbreaking attempt at a bio-social explanation of human consciousness remains today a seminal and inspiring account of the crucial importance of human communication for the social order. Sociologists, social psychologists and other social scientists can thus find in Mead's thinking the outline of a communicative social theory the implications of which are yet to be fully explored. The present book aims at offering an account of Mead's ideas such that the current generation of social practitioners may learn from Mead's proposals and eventually make use of them in their future work. Of course, one should not ask Mead a question he did not consider – this is why it is so important for us to take into account the social and intellectual context that frames his work. This is not to say, however, that we cannot learn from Mead how to solve the problems that we face today; it only means that the resolution of contemporary problems requires more than our predecessors can give us (and that they can give us a lot is exemplified by Mead's case). Mead did not simply rest upon the shoulders of giants – he used them to see further, and this was *his* achievement. This is what we, too, should try to do. In brief, it is this book's goal that we may all come to see further after engaging in a meaningful and enriching conversation with Mead.

The book falls into two major parts. The first part concerns Mead's ideas (chapters 2 to 5). The second part deals with the reception of these ideas by subsequent authors and analyses the contemporary relevance of Mead's work (chapters 6 to 8). Some brief comments on the internal organization of each part are in order. Chapter 2 next offers a discussion of Mead's personal and intellectual portrait. My aim is to provide, for readers without prior knowledge of Mead, a brief presentation of the major social and intellectual events that shaped Mead's life, with particular attention to the influence exercised by the city of Chicago upon his intellectual and civic activities. Chapter 2 is thus the only chapter whose rationale is to revolve around a historical narrative, even though I discuss various elements of his work by reference to the historical context (Mead's socio-psychological analysis of warfare as a response to World War I is a case in point); the remainder of the book follows an analytical perspective, discussing Mead's key ideas from the viewpoint of their conceptual origins, relations and implications. One should always keep in mind that there is a systematic relation uniting such otherwise disparate elements as Mead's discussion of the notion of 'conversation of gestures' within 'social acts' and his account of the communicative nature of the social order, or his ethical theory.

The first of the three chapters devoted to the analysis of Mead's ideas, chapter 3, begins with a detailed discussion of the concept of 'taking the role of the other'. This crucially important notion will be shown to play a strategic role within Mead's social psychology. The chapter unfolds by addressing other relevant conceptual elements such as the notions of 'gesture', of 'meaning' and of 'significant symbol', to arrive at the relation between linguistic communication and human consciousness. Chapter 4, in turn, deals with what is commonly considered to be Mead's chief contribution to contemporary social theory, namely his account of the self as a social emergent. Human subjectivity, our sense of who we are, is explained by Mead as emerging out of social experience – the human psyche and collective life are, Mead suggests, but different sides of the same coin. My discussion will proceed in three different steps: firstly, I introduce Mead's notions of 'consciousness', 'reflective intelligence' and 'mind'; secondly, I analyse his account of the two-stage process of childhood development ('play' and 'game'); finally, I close my excursus on Mead's conception of the social self with a presentation of the I–me distinction. Chapter 5, the last one to dwell on Mead's ideas, is devoted to two different issues: on the one hand, I examine the sociological and political aspects of Mead's thinking; on the other hand, I discuss Mead's theory of the act. In the concluding section of that chapter I present three fundamental Meadian ideas; these correspond approximately to the issues discussed in chapters 3 to 5, thus paving the way for the second part of the book.

In the following three chapters, 6 to 8, I examine the history of the reception of Mead's ideas by a large and varied group of social thinkers, so that the contemporary relevance of his contributions can be established. In a word, I wish to answer the questions: 'How did Mead's work influence the subsequent generations of social scientists?' and 'Why should one read Mead today?'. I believe that, by providing an answer to this pair of questions, additional light can be shed upon Mead's achievement. In other words, by moving beyond the scope of the context of Mead's life and texts one can better appreciate the relevance of his work for our present purposes. Thus in chapter 6 I examine the appropriation of Mead's ideas by the only sociological current that claims to be in a direct line of intellectual descent from Mead: symbolic interactionism. Although exceptionally fruitful from the point of view of empirical research, symbolic interactionism, it will be suggested, clearly departed from Mead's work in certain key aspects. A subsidiary claim of mine refers to the fact that some of the criticisms levelled against symbolic interactionism could be countered, provided that renewed attention is given to those aspects of Mead's work which certain influential symbolic interactionists (notably Herbert Blumer) tended to neglect.

The reception of Mead's work by other twentieth-century social scientists is the topic around which chapter 7 revolves. I begin by discussing the work of Arnold Gehlen, the author who should take the credit for introducing Mead's ideas in post-war Germany. My argument unfolds through the interpretations of Mead's thinking propounded by Jürgen Habermas, Hans Joas and Axel Honneth. The chapter ends with a discussion of the current appropriations of Mead's work by leading American sociologists, namely Randall Collins and Jeffrey Alexander. The final chapter deals with the contemporary relevance of Mead's theories. It does so by critically addressing four of its dimensions: the biological self, science, language and radical democracy – which will be my guidelines in the first section of that chapter. This will be followed by a section whose aim is to guide the reader through primary and secondary sources (an up-to-date, comprehensive list of which is provided at the end of the book).

In sum, my aim in what follows is to introduce the current generation of social sciences students, as well as the general public, to the
work of an author whose 'mind was a forum of discussion with itself',[30]
and whose work has inspired generations of thinkers across the globe.
I see no better way of paying homage to Mead than to engage him in
an imaginary conversation, through the writings he left us. Of course,
such a dialogue, far from being apologetic, must be critical and demanding – after all, there are many instances in which Mead's insights are
either insufficiently developed or have been proven wrong by subsequent research. Still, Mead's contribution to the understanding of the
problem of the individual mind in relation to social life arguably ranks
amongst the most valuable insights we have inherited from our classic
predecessors. And now I wish to turn to the context in which this contribution has developed.

2

Life and Work: 1863–1931

In this chapter my goal is to present the main episodes of Mead's intellectual history. Cities often provide the most privileged context in which to frame the biography of a social thinker. The close relation of Weber and Simmel to the city of Berlin at the turn of the century, or Durkheim's connection to *fin de siècle* Paris, are fine illustrations of what I have in mind. In Mead's case, too, there is an urban setting in which most of his life and work developed: the city of Chicago in the early decades of the twentieth century. Mead was not a Chicagoan by birth, however, nor did he grow up in the city. He was born in South Hadley, Massachusetts, on 27 February 1863. Six years later, his father, Hiram Mead, was appointed to a chair of theology at a Seminary in Oberlin, Ohio, and it was in this small New England town that George Mead spent his childhood, attending Oberlin College between 1880 and 1883. Before his move to Chicago in 1894, where he would remain until his death in 1931, Mead lived through a number of professional and personal formative experiences. These early experiences and Mead's mature engagement in Chicago's intellectual, social and political life should be considered the two single most important biographical contexts of his life.

The argument of this largely biographical chapter will unfold as follows. In a discussion of Mead's early intellectual development, the formative influence of two close friends, Henry Castle and John Dewey, deserves a special mention and will receive it. Mead's personal and intellectual development at Chicago will then follow. I will present his academic career in the philosophy department and his remarkable influence there despite his confessed difficulties in putting his thoughts into writing, his plans to publish a book on social psychology, and his mature discovery of the relativistic philosophies of Bergson and Whitehead – with an emphasis on his civic activities, a facet of Mead which is usually underplayed. Mead was not simply an academic thinker living in an ivory tower; during most of his life, he was also a committed citizen, making full use of his intellectual tools to cope with the social and political issues of his time.

The early years

One of the most important events in Mead's early years was without doubt his encounter with Henry Castle, a classmate from Oberlin College. As Mead acknowledged later, Castle was 'a larger part of my Oberlin life than all the rest put together; his friendship was more education than what beside the place afforded'.[1] Their relationship was motivated both by personal and by intellectual reasons; the latter included a 'common interest in philosophical affairs'[2] which was to shape Mead's early philosophical orientation. In the American college system of the 1880s, Noah Porter's *The Elements of Intellectual Science* (1871), a textbook version of his 1868 *The Human Intellect* (the most influential book on psychology published in America before William James' *The Principles of Psychology*), was standard reading for undergraduates taking a moral philosophy course. Oberlin College was no exception. Mead and Castle, however, were no great enthusiasts of Scottish moral philosophy. The two friends' reservations concerning this brand of moral philosophy were related to its approach to the doctrine of free will. As Castle's correspondence shows,[3] they were only too willing to show in the classroom their dissatisfaction with the logical contradictions of such a doctrine. The significance of this episode lies in Mead's open questioning of a philosophical tradition which combined Christian piety with Scottish moral philosophy. At a time when the natural sciences and Darwinism were challenging the Christian dominance of higher education in the USA, Mead's juvenile dissatisfaction with the traditional philosophy taught at Oberlin indicates that, in spite of being a pious young man (a characteristic he would retain for the rest of his life), Mead was nevertheless intellectually open to other explanations of the world.

Mead graduated from Oberlin College in the summer of 1883. Four years would pass before he met his friend Castle again. In the meantime, Mead tried to earn a living. After working first as a teacher at a high school in nearby Berlin Heights, in the spring of 1884 he began work as a surveyor in Minnesota for an extension of the Wisconsin Central Railroad, only to quit a few months later. Later he later took another surveyor position (for the Minneapolis and Pacific Railroad), which he abandoned again in early 1885. These work experiences did not appeal to him, interested as he was in pursuing a career in the world of letters, particularly in 'philosophical criticism and Literature';[4]

unfortunately, his lack of personal funds made such a goal almost impossible.

In January 1885, he started working as a private tutor in Minneapolis. While Mead was teaching preparatory students, his friend Castle sailed for Europe, to enrol on a philosophy course at the University of Berlin. This was not an uncommon thing for a young American to do. In the last quarter of the nineteenth century, thousands of American students studied at German universities, arguably the most respected ones in academia at the time.[5] Castle went to Berlin to study philosophy, but soon changed his mind and returned to America to pursue a career in law, despite Mead's advice to do otherwise. In early 1887, Castle enrolled at the Harvard Law School, a decision which proved to have profound consequences for Mead's own academic career. Mead visited his childhood friend soon after Castle arrived at Harvard and the two-day visit made quite an impact on him. In April that year he was asking Castle about Harvard application procedures. Mead's application was successful and in September he left Minneapolis for Cambridge, Massachusetts.

Once at Harvard, Mead had to give up his plans to enrol for Josiah Royce's course on Kant, since his German was not good enough. At the time, Royce was one of the chief intellectual figures of American academia and it was certainly a great disappointment for Mead not to be able to enrol. He did, however, enrol on other courses offered by Royce. As Castle wrote in a letter to his sister Helen: 'George has got all his courses settled, and has got work to do. He takes a course in ethics with Palmer, a course on Spinoza and Spencer with Royce and two Greek courses. The Kant course [with Royce] he will not take regularly, but expects to come in and listen.'[6] Another major figure at Harvard was William James, who taught psychology at first (the very first course on the subject in the US) and later on philosophy, when Mead himself was at Harvard. Contrary to what was assumed for many years, Mead never studied under James, although they did know each other quite well. James invited Mead to spend a summer teaching his son at his home at Chocorua, New Hampshire. As Mead explained to his friend Castle, 'Prof. James told me that he had several applications for the place but that I took care of myself so well in the examination that he wished me especially [for the position] as he could then have someone to whom he could talk metaphysics.'[7] By the end of that summer, for personal reasons only recently discovered,[8] Mead decided not to remain in Harvard for a second year. Instead, he fulfilled an old dream of his – to study at a German university.

Before seeing how Mead fared in Germany, it is necessary to make some brief comments on the institutional context of the development of academic life in the United States. From the second half of the nineteenth century to the first decades of the twentieth, the dramatic increase in college enrolments[9] reflected the huge private investment in higher education in those days. The University of Chicago is a good example of this situation. As with the universities of Cornell, Vanderbilt and Johns Hopkins, the creation of the University of Chicago was only possible due to John D. Rockefeller's thirty million dollars contribution. Small denominational colleges such as Oberlin College, where Mead studied, gradually gave way to large research universities.[10] The secularization of the American system of education, which continued up until the 1920s,[11] was one of the most significant traits of academic life during Mead's generation – a process he experienced in the most personal way. The conflict between religious conservatism, with its dogmatic explanations of the world, and the liberating scientific method of the natural sciences provides a crucially relevant background to Mead's early years. Also relevant is the process of differentiation within the American social sciences in the second half of the nineteenth century. To begin with, it is significant that the fields which were later to constitute the social sciences only started to appear in the 1870s. As we have just seen, physiological psychology as a discipline was first introduced by James, at Harvard. Another aspect of the process of differentiation in the social sciences concerns the profile of scholars in the last decades of the nineteenth century. According to Roscoe Hinkle, two different groups could be distinguished in this generation. One was traditionally oriented, and hence less motivated to differentiate new fields of research; the other comprised scholars willing to break with traditional disciplinary boundaries. The example adduced by Hinkle to illustrate this second group of academics in psychology was Stanley Hall (a friend of Dewey), who was in the 'vanguard of men trained in the new German physiological psychology with its laboratory emphasis'.[12]

'By the rarest piece of good luck in the world', as Castle put it, Mead met Hall by chance, in Germany, in the autumn of 1888, soon after his arrival. In fact Hall helped to dispel Mead's doubts concerning where and what to study in such a recent discipline. This casual encounter triggered Mead's decision to specialize, not in philosophy, but in physiological psychology; for, as his friend Castle stated,

> George [Mead] thinks he must make a speciality of this branch, because in America, where poor, bated, unhappy Christianity, trembling for its life, claps the gag into the mouth of Free Thought . . . he thinks it would be hard for him to get a chance to utter any ultimate philosophical opinions savoring of independence. In Physiological Psychology, on the other hand, he has a harmless territory in which he can work quietly without drawing down upon himself the anathema and excommunication of all-potent Evangelicalism.[13]

Mead's decision to specialize in this emergent field of research seems, then, to have been motivated by the wish to develop his naturalistic and evolutionary insights in an area where he could avoid direct confrontation with the religious orthodoxy. Science, whose method resorted to human intelligence to test working hypotheses, could then be reconciled with morals. His conscious move, in 1888, to pursue a career in physiological psychology rather than in philosophy seems to mark a crucial moment: one can see him adopting, for the first time, a scientific outlook in his approach to human affairs – from the origins of human conscience to the nature of the moral order.

During his stay in Germany, Mead lived and studied in two different locations. First he studied at the University of Leipzig, where he took several philosophy courses during the winter semester of 1888–9. One of these courses (Fundamentals of Metaphysics) was offered by Wilhelm Wundt, one of the founding fathers of psychology as a scientific discipline. Partly through dissatisfaction with the way this first semester went and partly owing to his encounter with Hall, Mead did not stay long in Leipzig. In March 1889 he moved to Berlin, where he enrolled at the prestigious Humboldt University. He then had the chance of studying under Wilhelm Dilthey; his renowned lectures on ethics had a profound effect upon the young Mead – so much so that he decided to undertake a doctoral dissertation under Dilthey's supervision. According to the letters Mead wrote to Castle, his intention was to reformulate Kant's conception of space from the point of view of physiological psychology. In other words, Mead rejected the Kantian thesis that space is a certain kind of intuition; in his opinion, space should be seen as 'a construction of our eye . . . the three dimensions rest simply upon the optic nerve and the sense of touch and especially the hand'.[14] He never completed this PhD project, however – a major reason for this being an invitation from Dewey, at the beginning of the summer of 1891, to join him at the University of Michigan in Ann Arbor. The new post as instructor of psychology there required Mead to teach physiological psychology. As he described it to Castle, it was: 'a course in the History of Phil.[losophy] and half a course in Kant – and another in [the theory of] Evolution.'[15]

After marrying Helen Castle, his best friend's sister, in Berlin on 1 October 1891, Mead sailed back to the United States with his new wife. In the following year the couple had their first and only child, Henry Castle Mead. From the two and a half years he spent in Germany, Mead gained not only a sound scientific background in the emerging discipline of physiological psychology, but also a profound sympathy for the socialist movement, especially at a municipal level. Enriched with its progressive ideas and ideals, he settled in Ann Arbor. The influence of Dewey on Mead during this period was very significant. Mead's usage of Dewey's ideas, and in particular of his version of Hegelianism, can be seen on various occasions. For instance, when Mead writes that 'the body and soul are but two sides of one thing, and that the gulf between them is only the expression of the fact that our life does not yet realize the ideal of what our social life will be',[16] he is conveying an idea originally formulated by Dewey, a functionalism according to which the life process should be understood as having two interrelated aspects, the physical and the mental. Social life is thus seen as an organic whole, which expresses itself both through nature and through human beings: when the latter act cooperatively upon the former in order to accomplish their goals, life acquires its social character. It is thus not surprising that Mead did not hesitate to follow Dewey when the latter decided to accept an offer, in 1894, from the newly opened University of Chicago. In the autumn of that year, Mead became an assistant professor in the Department of Philosophy chaired by Dewey, starting a relationship with the university and its city that would last for over thirty-five years. This relationship is the leitmotiv of the remainder of this chapter. Before we proceed, however, a word is needed to signal a tragic and unexpected event that affected Mead in the most profound way. I refer to the demise in 1895 of his childhood friend, Henry Castle, in a steamship collision in the North Sea. Throughout the rest of his life, Mead would always look back at his friendship with Castle as a deeply felt loss.

Mead in Chicago

At the beginning of the last century, Chicago was a rapidly growing metropolis and home to one of the world's most dynamic universities. In political terms, the 'windy city' was an exciting and challenging terrain for someone who, like Mead, was interested in radical social reform, particularly at a local level: the social integration of immigrants, the labour vs. capital conflicts, educational issues and the rights of women exemplify the sort of problems at the top of the political agenda in the early decades of the twentieth century. Mead's involvement in the Immigrants' Protective League (which he helped to found in 1908), his participation in a citizens' committee established to mediate the so-called 'garment strike' of 1910,[17] and his long-term membership both of the City Club of Chicago[18] and of the University of Chicago Settlement,[19] are examples of his belief that the 'study and work' of reform go hand in hand. Chicago was no less interesting intellectually than it was in political terms.

Of particular relevance for understanding Mead's place in American thought is the philosophical tradition of classical pragmatism, inaugurated by Charles Sanders Peirce and developed by James, Dewey and numerous others. In Mead's case, his allegiance to pragmatism casts light on two crucial dimensions of his life and work. On the one hand, the very term 'pragmatism', with its Greek root *pragma* ('thing done'),[20] hints at the worldliness of Mead's philosophy, oriented as it is to the resolution of the problematic situations in certain parts of the 'world that is there'. On the other hand, such an orientation to 'practicality' was guided by a genuine trust in the possibilities of science. This trust is not to be confused with scientism or an endorsement of science's neutrality to value; for the pragmatists, and particularly Mead, were only too aware of the social embeddedness of science. This said, one cannot understand Mead's position in intellectual history only by reference to pragmatism.

If one looks at Mead's writings at the turn of the century, 'Hegelianism', understood as a 'method of thought', was at the very centre of his agenda. A case in point is his 1901 paper 'A New Criticism of Hegelianism: Is it Valid?', a book review in which Mead expresses his position with great clarity. The author of the book in question, Charles D'Arcy, attempts to formulate a definition of human subjectivity which could answer the question: 'How can our knowledge of other personalities be given objective validity?'[21] D'Arcy suggests that an insurmountable chasm separates individual consciousnesses[22] and that our knowledge of physical objects is more objective than our knowledge of personalities.[23] To this Mead retorts that from the perspective of a 'social consciousness within which selves arise these chasms have the positive significance of the points of reconstruction[, for the] analysis of consciousness reveals an essentially social nature of the self'.[24] A philosophy aimed at producing objective solutions for problems that arise in action must, in the case of the psychical, state the method by which the self meets and solves these difficulties, rather than fall into the trap of a metaphysical quest for a perennially subjective being. Hegel's influence is still very much present at this time, but it would be a mistake to infer from this fact that Mead supported some sort of metaphysical speculation about ever-subjective entities. Hegel's dialectics is, in Mead's reading, a useful tool for coping with the problems of action humanity has to face. It is a method of thought, whose experimental scientific potential was not adequately developed by Hegel himself.

The main reason behind Mead's early adoption of Hegelianism was, of course, Dewey's own enthusiasm for Hegel. Mead's texts on education and pedagogy constitute a good example of Dewey's influence over him. Dewey's educational theory (as presented, for instance, in the widely celebrated 1900 book *School and Society*) not only gave rise to an influential current of pedagogical thinking, but was also the driving force behind the University Elementary School, founded by Dewey himself in 1896. This 'Laboratory School', as it came to be known later, was intended to give concrete shape to Dewey's progressive educational theses – a project the Meads joined in with great enthusiasm, enrolling young Henry in the school. It should thus come as no surprise that, as far as his pedagogical writings were concerned, Mead was heavily indebted to Dewey. For instance, in 1896 Mead can be seen asking his colleagues whether a child's mind can be conceived of as an 'empty country into which the educator can go, like the manager of a telegraph company, and put wires where he will'.[25] The rejection of such a view stems from Mead's objection to adopting work as the main principle of education. Instead, the school should adopt the notion of play as its key principle, in the sense that the stimuli provoked by the surrounding objects must be so arranged that they will 'answer to the natural growth of the child's organism, both as respects the objects he becomes successively interested in and the relations which they have to each other in the life process that he will have to carry out'.[26] From the beginning, then, Mead conceived of education as a means of intelligent control over the child's natural process of development, rejecting both an authoritarian model of inculcation of information and a model where the absence of discipline prevents intelligence from guiding the child's impulses. According to the pragmatists' progressive model of education, the school cannot be separated from the home, since both are fundamental social spheres where the child's development takes place.

A second example of Mead's early Hegelianism and of Dewey's influence is to be found in his writings on social reform. The Hegelian character of Mead's reformism shows in the assumption that social phenomena possess an intelligible nature, and that this nature is available to the human mind. In other words, the scientific method, as an expression of human intelligence (in fact Mead and other pragmatists called it the 'method of intelligence'), can throw light on the laws that govern social events. As we have seen above, one of the consequences of Mead's stay in Germany was his profound esteem for municipal socialism. It is therefore only natural that Mead chose this sort of political solution to illustrate his social reformism in the 1899 article 'The Working Hypothesis in Social Reform'. Rejecting socialist approaches to social reform of a utopian or 'programmistic' character, Mead nevertheless believed that the socialist ideal of effecting 'by constructive legislation radical changes that will lead to greater social equality'[27] was perfectly valid. His rejection of utopian socialism was tantamount to a rejection of grandiose schemes of general social and political change; he favoured a scientifically driven, piece-meal reformism. Instead of attempting to change the world, which often leads to tyranny and oppression, Mead and the pragmatists aimed at solving concrete social and political problems in such a way as to foster democracy 'as a way of life'. Science, Mead thought during his early Chicago years, could be the best method for solving moral and political issues. This faith in a scientific approach to social reform would eventually diminish as a result of the greatest military conflict of Mead's generation, World War I.

However, before turning to Mead's reaction to that conflict, it might be profitable to examine, if briefly, another area of his activity which reflects the formative importance of Dewey's early Hegelianism: Mead's writings on social psychology, the field of research where he made arguably his most original and influential contributions. Mead taught courses on comparative psychology and on the methodology of psychology both at Michigan and at Chicago. His offering of a widely popular course on social psychology at Chicago not only explains his life-long interest in the subject, but also helps one to understand his influence over sociology students (one should not forget that Mead was a member of the philosophy department). The articles he published at that time already showed the social conception of human subjectivity that was to give his theories their distinctive character.[28] At an early stage, however, Mead's position was not that different from that of Dewey. It would take a few more years, until the early 1910s, for Mead to develop a social-psychological theory with linguistic and phylogenetic implications enabling it to supersede that of Dewey – or of any other pragmatist, for that matter. In 1905, owing to a personal conflict with the President of the University of Chicago, William Harper, Dewey and the latter's wife decided to abandon Chicago and move to New York, where Columbia University had offered Dewey a position. Mead and Dewey, however, would remain close friends for the rest of their lives.

Mead's life in Chicago was as exciting as the life of the city itself. He was extremely busy trying to balance an academic career of writing and lecturing on social psychology and educational theory with his numerous social reformist activities. This is the context in which one should interpret Mead's decision not to publish a book on social psychology in 1911 – which would prove eventually to be the closest he ever came to publishing a book. Recently made available to the general public,[29] this long-forgotten volume provides us with a clear picture of Mead's intellectual interests around the 1910s. Mead selected for publication eighteen essays on social psychology, comparative psychology and philosophy of education, of which nine were still unpublished. That he chose to include ten essays on educational issues, four of which were unpublished, reveals the centrality of this topic for his social psychology. On the whole, the eighteen chapters that comprise this volume are an eloquent testimony of his early social-psychological and educational theses. Mead, however, had strong reasons for not wanting to proceed with the publication of the *Essays on Psychology*, principally in the theoretical development undergone by his social-psychological thinking during this period. The 'social turn' in Mead's theory of perception and conception of human consciousness around 1910 explains, in my view, why he did not want to see this volume published. It is only natural that he did not wish to associate his name with a social psychology to which he no longer fully subscribed. There is also an additional motive of a circumstantial nature. Mead's reformist activities at the time were extremely time-consuming, which might have prevented him from revising the galley proofs he received from the publisher in early 1911. He was then editing, coordinating and publishing a 300-page report on vocational education in Chicago, and, as hinted above, he was also actively engaged in a number of other voluntary activities. Finally, the nature of Mead's intellectual edifice is perhaps a third reason why the *Essays* were never published during his lifetime: his was indeed, paradoxically, a system in a state of flux.

The later years

A few years later, on the other side of the Atlantic, the assassination of Archduke Francis Ferdinand of Austria–Hungary by a Serbian nationalist precipitated a war of unprecedented scale and ferocity. Europe was divided into two contending parts: between 1914 and 1918, the 'Central Powers' (Germany, Austria–Hungary and the Ottoman Empire) fought against the 'Allies' (a coalition of countries led by Great Britain, France and Russia), engulfing Europe in a conflict which extended to both sides of the Atlantic with America's entry into the war in April 1917. World War I constituted a challenge for early twentieth-century intellectuals and scientists. It is fair to say that a whole generation of social thinkers, including sociology's classic figures, was offered the chance to supersede particularistic and non-scientific prejudices in the name of scientific objectivity and impartiality. Most of them failed to meet that challenge, but this was not true of Mead. His wartime personal correspondence and political writings, some of them still unpublished, reveal a social scientist deeply concerned with the humanitarian consequences of war, yet willing to provide a scientific explanation of the causes and nature of that human tragedy. In this respect, as we will see in chapter 5, Mead's social-psychological explanation of the fusion of the two phases of the self in patriotic moments is of particular relevance.

Only too aware of the difficulties of putting into practice his political ideal of rational democratic deliberation, Mead devoted the last decade of his career to the study of epistemology and philosophy of science. In this respect, the influence of Alfred North Whitehead and Henry Bergson cannot be underestimated. It should be emphasized that Mead was becoming increasingly dissatisfied with the Hegelianism he had espoused in the early years of his career. When, in the late 1910s, he discovered the relativistic theories of Bergson and Whitehead, he found philosophical answers to many of the questions his early Hegelianism was no longer able to provide. In his view, the existence of one single absolute perspective (presupposed by absolute idealism) precludes the objectivity of individual perspectives, as well as evolution, novelty and creativity. On the contrary, Mead's social theory of human conscious-ness and Whitehead's relativistic philosophy share the same emphasis on the 'objectivity of perspectives'.[30] What Mead wishes to select from the latter's proposal is its 'conception of nature as an organization of perspectives, which are there in nature'.[31] Individual perspectives emerge from a social perspective which, in turn, transcends the mere collection of individual perspectives. But how can one secure the objec-tivity of individual perspectives? For Mead, the answer to this question lies in a pragmatic test. An individual perspective, understood as an organization of events, is considered to be objective or real if it leads to the consummation of an act that was previously inhibited. At this point it is necessary to bear in mind that Mead conceives of the act as consisting of four stages. Firstly, there is an impulse, in the sense of a physiological predisposition of the organism to respond to a given stimulus; secondly, the organism perceives either an object or a part of the surrounding environment; thirdly, the organism manipulates the perceived object, either physically (e.g. an apple) or intellectually (e.g. a past event); fourthly, the organism attributes a certain value to the object in question, thereby consummating the act. This is the defining element of Mead's model of action, and an important element of his system of philosophy.

This system of philosophy is the subject of my book, and the present chapter has attempted to show that there is a life behind the texts of an author. Indeed, the work of any given thinker is better understood if a reference is made to the world in which he or she lived. In Mead's case, a substantial part of that world was the city of Chicago at the turn of the century, with its vibrant new university and its chaotic yet thrill-ing social life. The remainder of the book will discuss Mead's ideas, particularly his social-psychological theories. One of the most fascinat-ing aspects of Mead's thinking lies in its being 'in-the-making'. It is not by chance that its central motif is the idea of dialogue; for its cognitive import, its social and cooperative nature, and its fluidity all concur in characterizing Mead's philosophy not so much as a system as a state of flux.

3

Mead's Social Psychology: Basic Concepts

One of the most suggestive metaphors about the social nature of human beings is found in Daniel Defoe's character, Robinson Crusoe. The story of Robinson Crusoe, a British sailor lost on an island off the coast of Venezuela for almost three decades and having for company only a native he calls Man Friday, has seized the imagination of every generation since its publication in the mid-eighteenth century. I would like to begin this chapter by asking: could Crusoe have constructed homes as he did, built the same artefacts, and raised goats and crops, had he been left on that island as a small child and not as a grown adult? What Mead's social psychology gives us are the reasons why the answer to this question must be negative. That is, Mead teaches us that Crusoe was only able to do so because he transported with him, to the island, the accumulated social experiences of an adult man; a newborn child would not even have survived the first week in such a hostile environment, let alone be able to develop his self. The metaphor of the adventures of Robinson Crusoe thus seems to make a useful illustration for Mead's social-psychological arguments – an illustration he himself used in his classes.

Admittedly, the idea that the sense of who and what we are develops from the outside in rather than from the inside out is still difficult to accept for most of us. This shows how ingrained in the public mind the traditional Cartesian view is that our self is the product of our body, and of our brain in particular. Mead follows a different route. For him, one can aspire to understand the origins and nature of the human self only if one conceives of it as the product of social life. The starting point for Mead, then, is not the individual self, rational and driven by some fundamental impulses. Mead's communicative social theory begins instead with the social experience through which individual selves eventually emerge. Rather than an act performed by a solitary rational individual, it is an interaction between organisms who will later become selves that is the foundation stone of Mead's philosophy.

In this chapter my argument will unfold as follows. I will begin by trying to show the strategic position that the concept of 'taking the attitude of the other' occupies in Mead's social psychology. For Mead, if the cortex is the physiological condition for the development of human society, it is due to our ability to take the role of others that we become objects to ourselves, i.e. we become selves. The self emerges within a social and linguistic process whose symbolic nature cannot be overemphasized. Vocal gestures provide the medium for social organization insofar as they allow the self to arise in conduct. These gestures become significant symbols through role-taking: when an individual utters a vocal gesture, this leads to a certain response in his interlocutor; the response is the symbol of that act. In turn, a significant symbol emerges every time a vocal gesture arouses a similar response both in the individual uttering it and in the individual listening to it. The human mind, then, is not to be equated with the brain; far from confining it to the mental processes that take place within individuals, Mead conceives of the mind as emerging from the relations of individuals to objects, physical and social alike. Mead's conception of social life is that of a cooperative, symbolically mediated process in which language performs the crucial function of social coordination. By construing language as the organizational principle of human social life, Mead wishes to rule out alternative explanations, which tend to ignore or downplay the social and symbolic aspects of human experience. Mead's alternative, as we shall see, points to the need for a scientific reconstruction of two intertwined processes – the historical–phylogenetic evolution of the human species and the developmental–ontogenetic growth of every human individual. An example of the complementary character of these two processes will then be found in Mead's much neglected analysis of the various 'moods of language', in which several forms of linguistic interaction are thought of both as stages of social evolution and as phases of the linguistic act. The chapter will end with a discussion of the two central functions performed by language in Mead's communicative social theory: it is, simultaneously, the basic principle of human social organization and the principle responsible for the emergence of the human mind.

Taking the role of the other

For Mead, human beings live in a world made of objects. Most objects around us are physical: a pen or a mobile 'phone are possible examples of what Mead calls 'objects of immediate experience'.[1] We can grab them, feel them, use them. Moreover, Mead suggests that human beings are also to be considered as objects, only of a different sort: the reflective intelligence of the human self makes it a social object. Social objects (i.e. human beings) are distinguished from physical ones through their ability to reflect upon the surrounding environment, including other social objects. Mead's interest lies in reconstructing the process through which human beings become the most important objects to themselves.[2] How does this occur? The answer to this question leads us directly to one of Mead's most important concepts, the notion of 'taking the role or the attitude of the other' ('role' and 'attitude' will be used interchangeably). I relate to my fellow colleague, Mead would say, by taking his attitude towards me. As he puts it: 'we are what we are in our relationship to other individuals through taking the attitude of the other individuals toward ourselves so that we stimulate ourselves by our own gesture'.[3] Mead believes we interact with physical and social objects in a parallel way. Resorting to the same psychological mechanism of taking the attitude of the other, we put ourselves in the role of the other, be it a pen or a friend. Of course, communication in the former case is rather limited, while in the latter it is of great complexity.

The notion of 'taking the role or attitude of the other' is Mead's version of the old philosophical concept of reflectivity, which appears for the first time as the founding principle of philosophy in Descartes's work. But, unlike Descartes's 'Cogito, ergo sum' ('I am thinking, therefore I exist'), Mead's conception of reflectivity is not that of an innate capacity but of one learned through social experience. As suggested above, Mead argues that the 'self has the characteristic that it is an object to itself, and that characteristic distinguishes it from other objects and from the body'.[4] In other words, the self distinguishes itself from other objects, either physical or social, when it sees itself as an independent entity; moreover, Mead stresses that the self should not be equated with the body; for, while we can see, say, our feet, we cannot see the body as a whole. We do, however, experience ourselves as a whole. It is precisely this sort of self-awareness that distinguishes the self. The self is thus simultaneously subject and object.

While interacting with other social objects, the self engages in what Mead refers to as 'role-taking'. Again, here too, the self is simultaneously subject and object. There is one important difference, though. In this case, the self reflects upon itself (sees itself as an object) through the eyes of the other, so to speak. The self adopts the standpoint or attitude of its partner in communication in the sense of importing to its own conduct a tendency to respond to a certain type of stimulus just as the other would. Reflectivity, according to Mead, has two different action levels: the subjective, where the self sees itself as an object, and the intersubjective, where the self takes the attitude of the communication partner. In Mead's philosophy the intersubjective model of reflectivity takes clear precedence, as the subjective is defined in dialogical terms. Recovering a Platonic–Aristotelian insight, Mead suggests that thinking is a sort of 'inner conversation'.[5] Human intelligence is thus inherently reflective, and this reflectivity is of a dialogical character. The very monologue that occurs in our mind is, according to Mead, nothing but a subjective form of dialogue.

Contrary to what the expression 'taking the role of the other' might suggest, Mead does not conceive of this psychological mechanism as a dramatic process involving the representation of social roles; rather, for him, role-taking is a cognitive process as much as it is a social and biological one. It is a social phenomenon insofar as it takes place only in a social group; for, as Mead explains, 'selves exist only in relation to other selves, as the organism as a physical object exists only in its relation to other physical objects'.[6] Taking the attitude of the other further implies that what is imported into one's conduct are not complex social roles, but behavioural dispositions to respond to a certain stimulus, roughly, as other individuals would. In this sense, even if self-consciousness is a dramatic affair to begin with, later on, as it develops into the abstract process of thought, the 'features and intonations of the dramatis personae fade out and the emphasis falls upon the meaning of the inner speech'.[7] As we shall see, this emphasis by Mead on the behavioural and cognitive character of role-taking is at variance with the prevalent conception among symbolic interactionists, who claim nevertheless to be in a direct line of intellectual descent from Mead.

Mead's notion of role-taking performs yet another important function in his social psychology: it is the behavioural mechanism behind the 'functional differentiation through language',[8] the principle of social organization that distinguishes human vertebrates from other animal species. If the other, lower animals (e.g. ants or bees) rely on physiological differentiation as the principle around which their social life is organized, Mead suggests that the social organization characteristic of the human species revolves around 'communication involving participation in the other'.[9] The principle of human social organization is language, a distinctively human ability that combines cognition, social experience and symbolic import to a degree of complexity unmatched by any other animal species on earth. In particular, the evolution of the human species is due to the combination of two orders of factors: firstly, the experience of communal life motivated by social impulses; secondly, the development of the cortex of the vertebrate central nervous system. The latter is a necessary (physiological) condition for the development of the human species, but it is not a sufficient condition: 'If the cortex has become an organ of social conduct, and has made possible the appearance of social objects, it is because the individual has become a self, that is, an individual who organizes his own response by the tendencies on the part of others to respond to his act.'[10] What Mead wishes to rule out is the notion that the development of the human cortex is the sole reason for the development of science, the arts, technology and every other achievement that distinguishes humankind. Mead's alternative explanation points to the pivotal role played by social experience as the triggering phenomenon of the behavioural mechanism of taking the roles of others and, subsequently, of the emergence of the self. This is how the self becomes a distinctive feature of human vertebrates.

I will return to this important issue in a moment, but now I wish to discuss an additional feature of Mead's conception of 'taking the role of the other': the human ability to imagine or anticipate the other's likely response to our gesture. This anticipatory character of Mead's notion of role-taking is better understood by reference to his concept of 'object' and his four-phased model of action, which I have introduced at the end of the previous chapter. The self perceives at distance a certain physical object, whose contact expectations can be fulfilled only at a later moment. For example, I see a chair and I move across the room to sit on it. I thus have a few seconds to adjust my behaviour to the behaviour of the object before me, in this case a chair. This adjustment allows me to import some of the qualities of the chair (say, its form and resistance), so that, by the time I sit on the chair, those qualities will already be in my organism. In this way, before I sit on the chair I consider whether or not it will hold my weight and I anticipate that it will. The same is true, of course, in relation to social objects, only in this case the complexity of the anticipatory role-taking is far greater and predisposes us to mistakes.

We have examined so far the notions of 'object' and 'role-taking'; my aim has been to introduce the most basic elements of Mead's social theory of the self. There are, however, several other crucial concepts without which Mead's social psychology cannot be understood. In order to examine these, I now turn to Mead's explanation of the process of development in the human species. In this respect, a concept emerges as particularly important. I refer to the notion of 'gesture', which Mead borrows from Wundt.[11]

Gestures and the 'social act'

Social experience is the sole precondition Mead allows in explaining the origins and development of human consciousness. However, in order to avoid an untenable circularity, he needs to explain how primates achieved the primordial role-taking conduct that preceded the properly human capacity of 'taking the attitude of the other'. He does that by combining the two lines of reasoning adduced above. To begin with, Mead signals the importance of the development of the human cortex: this was the material cause for the 'appearance of distinctively human conduct'.[12] Yet this physiological development does not by itself explain how human conduct evolved. It was, so to speak, the necessary condition for the development of the role-taking attitude in humans. However, to look for the sufficient condition, one has to turn to another physiological feature, now of a social character. Mead points to the role of impulses which 'involve or require social situations and relations for their satisfaction'.[13] These fundamental social impulses and needs (such as the reproductive impulse, the parental impulse, or the impulse for neighbourliness) constitute the foundation of the general process of social differentiation. As we shall see, other thinkers working in Chicago at the same time as Mead were developing complex sociological models, drawing from this notion of a set of 'social forces'. I am thinking of Albion Small, the founder of the sociology department, and W. I. Thomas, probably the most important Chicago sociologist in the 1910s. Mead's employment of the notion of 'social impulses' is thus a sign of the social pragmatism he shared with most of his colleagues in Chicago. Let us now return to Mead's analysis of the role performed by these impulses.

By virtue of the social character of their impulses, the behaviour of individual organisms, such as our primate ancestors, is always a component of the social life of the group. Mead's favoured concept to explain this particular developmental situation is the notion of 'conversation of gestures (or attitudes)' within 'social acts'.[14] Imagine a group of primates, endowed with the socio-physiological impulses that bring them together in cooperative activities. When at least two of these primates engage in social interaction, Mead suggests we have a 'social act' before us. The movement or attitude of one primate that serves as a stimulus to the other primate involved in this social act is a 'gesture'. As the interaction proceeds, the primates exchange these gestures back and forth: the act of each primate becomes the stimulus for the other to respond to. This 'conversation of gestures' only takes place, Mead argues, because the primates in question have impulses that require a social situation for their satisfaction. Of course, the variety of social acts is immense, for there are numerous types of social impulses: the social acts range from an act of love to the most destructive form of violence, from a simple interaction between two individuals to a gathering of a whole group of them. What one has to bear in mind is the fact that the gestures comprised in such social acts, when performed by non-human individuals, are not significant, that is, 'the response of another organism to it does not indicate to the organism making it what the other organism is responding to'.[15] In other words, Mead distinguishes between the 'unconscious conversation of gestures', reserved for the most elementary forms of social interaction,[16] and the 'conscious conversation of gestures', which arises when gestures become signs. The evolutionary passage from an unconscious to a conscious conversation of gestures could not have occurred without the social experience of language, Mead argues.

I now wish to discuss in detail how Mead reconstructs the emergence of the conscious conversation of gestures or communication. For Mead, not all gestures can become signs. For a gesture to carry a definite meaning, both for the individual making it and for the individual responding to it, it must call forth a similar response for both individuals engaged in that particular social act. The only type of gesture that releases a similar stimulus both to its sender and to the receiver is the 'vocal gesture'. The oral nature of vocal gestures permits the individual who is uttering them to listen to them as much as the other individuals do. It is this peculiar feature that explains why only vocal gestures allow us to take 'the attitudes of the other persons into our own conduct'.[17] Moreover, articulated sounds are the most adequate mechanism for self-monitoring our performance. An example might be of use here. Let us go back to our group of primates and think of two individuals engaging in a social act. The male utters a certain vocal gesture, which is heard both by him and by his female interlocutor. By doing this, he is able to put himself in her role, i.e. he is able to imagine what her response will be to his vocal gesture. And he is able to imagine this because he is listening to his words, just as she is. The speaking primate thus takes the role of the listening primate. Then she speaks back, and the opposite occurs: since she can also listen to herself speak, she is able to take his role. She can imagine how he will respond to her vocal gesture because this particular type of gesture is available to both speaker and listener. For Mead, meaning was born when, at some point in evolution, the speaking primate learned how to respond to a vocal gesture in a similar way to its interlocutor. The consciousness of meaning emerged when primates learned how to take the role of the other; with reflective intelligence, primates began to perceive and manipulate the objects around them in a radically different way – they could now see the 'inside' of things, i.e. their abstract properties. Living in an empirical world inhabited by physical and social objects, primates become aware of this reflective capacity via an individual other. The birth of the self is thus dialogical.

Meaning and the significant symbol

According to Mead's theory of phylogenesis, language emerged when individuals gained awareness of the social import of the vocal gestures they uttered. What turns vocal gestures into elements of something that one can properly call a language? For a vocal stimulus to become significant, two conditions must be met: firstly, the individual responds to his own stimulus as the other individuals do; secondly, 'this response within one's self . . . is one which is a stimulus to the individual as well as a response'.[18] Only then does a 'significant symbol' arise. Such a symbol has a certain signification attached: it has a certain meaning. For Mead's arguments the relevance of these two concepts – 'significant symbol' and 'meaning' – demands a closer look.

To begin with, he emphasizes that significant symbols can only emerge in social interactions. The meaning of a gesture in any given social act is equated with the 'consciousness of response or readiness to respond'[19] on the part of the acting individual. Such a consciousness of meaning has the social act as its behavioural condition. Mead asserts: '[t]he significant gesture or symbol always presupposes for its significance the social process of experience and behaviour in which it arises'.[20] In other words, natural languages and symbols are common to social groups. Yet Mead is keen to point out that they are also imported into individual conduct and personalities. Significant symbols, therefore, are the basis for the individual's abstraction and reflective thinking as well as for his interaction and participation in social life. Take the example of someone waiting alone for a friend in a park. While sitting there, she thinks about her life: how her day went at work, her expectations about the upcoming meeting, and so on. Albeit physically alone, in thinking, she uses significant symbols; however, as soon as her friend arrives, she will use them to talk to him. As this example shows, both reflective thinking and linguistic communication require 'significant symbols'. Still, it is worth noting at this point that the expression 'symbolic interaction' was not coined by Mead himself but by one of his students, Herbert Blumer, who will be discussed in the chapter dedicated to the sociological current of symbolic interactionism.

Secondly, the defining feature of a significant symbol is its symbolic nature. Mead refuses any introspectivist approach, though. For him, the language symbol is 'simply a significant or conscious gesture'; its interpretation is an 'external, overt, physical, physiological process going on in the actual field of social experience'.[21] How does Mead define a symbol? First of all, it is not to be confused with the notion of meaning. Mead describes the logical structure of meaning as an inner triad made of the gesture of the first organism, the responding gesture of the second organism and the 'resultant' of the social act. The response of the second organism to the gesture of the first organism is the interpretation of that gesture – this response brings out the meaning. Meaning is thus implicit in the structure of the social act; as such, meaning is to be found 'objectively there in social conduct'.[22] Mead uses the example of the footprint of a bear to explain his argument. The footprint is the symbol of a bear: when we stumble on such a footprint we associate that imprinted piece of mud with the passing of a bear at some previous moment. We might be afraid, not of the footprint but of what it means – the bear. So the footprint is the symbol, the bear is its meaning (i.e. the 'resultant' of the social act), and to be able to identify such a symbol as leading to such a meaning is the distinctive feature of human intelligence. Individuals thus create symbols to indicate, to themselves as well as to the other members of the group, the implications of a certain object or gesture. In a sense, then, symbolization creates objects. The piece of mud only becomes a 'footprint' when an individual looks at it and interprets it as meaning 'bear'. Such an object could not have existed if it were not for the social context in which that process of symbolization occurs. There are at least two implications one can draw from this conception of symbolization. Firstly, as Mead puts it, language 'makes possible the existence of the appearance of that situation or object, for it is a part of the mechanism whereby that situation or object is created'.[23] Secondly, the meaning of a certain object or gesture pre-exists the consciousness of meaning: it exists in the behavioural structure that relates individuals and the environment in which they live. Human conduct structures this relation so that, according to Mead, meaning is neither linguistically constituted nor a given datum.

Thirdly, in terms of its implications for Mead's general argument, I would like to emphasize the sociological consequences of the concept of 'significant symbol'. Mead's conception of society and social cooperation cannot be understood without reference to significant symbols. Complex, large-scale social life is possible only because human beings developed significant language. Mead's 'principle of social integration and organization in terms of rational selves'[24] rests upon the human ability for symbolization: '[f]or effective cooperation one has to have the symbols by means of which the responses can be carried out, so that getting a significant language is of first importance'.[25] As we have seen, this sharing of the responses of others is what distinguishes the unconscious conversation of gestures from conscious communication. Self-stimulation is barely present in the former, while it plays a decisive role in the latter. In sum, Mead's account of phylogeny, and of the evolutionary process of the emergence of human language in particular, offers this plausible explanation for a crucial transition in human evolution: the vocal gesture is given the decisive function of enabling humans, by responding to their own vocal gestures, to become objects to themselves.[26]

Language and the mind

We are now equipped to examine Mead's treatment of language, the social activity whose symbolic nature paved the way for the development of the human mind, and we should do this starting from the need for a word to describe Mead's methodological stance regarding the scientific study of natural languages. He rejects both the objectivistic approach of Watsonian behaviourism, which reduced subjective consciousness to purely behaviourist terms, and introspectionism, which made the opposite error of studying language as an originally subjective affair. In Mead's view, the 'study of the process of language or speech – its origins and development – is a branch of social psychology, because it can be understood only in terms of the social processes of behaviour within a group of interacting individuals'.[27] It is a naturalistic and socially minded perspective that Mead favours in the study of the emergence of language. In Mead's account of phylogeny, language emerged as a social cooperative activity performed by individual organisms whose conduct comprehended vocal gestures endowed with meaning. There is no original pure mind at the outset; for Mead the beginning is biological and social. What is, in his view, the sociophysiological mechanism which explains the emergence of language most adequately? As outlined above, Mead suggests that language has emerged when individuals gained awareness of the social import of the vocal gestures they uttered. The behavioural mechanism involved in this process was not imitation, as many thinkers before Mead have proposed. He did not find that the impulse for imitation was adequate to account for the process of language acquisition. Consider the case of the conversation of gestures. If one were to rely on the imitative impulse as the behavioural explanation for responding to a gesture, this response would never go beyond the threshold of mere reproduction. As Mead observes: 'the sensitive experience . . . cannot be a stimulus simply to reproduce what is seen and heard; it is rather a stimulus for the carrying out of the organic process'.[28] Mead's alternative explanation points to the human ability to take the role of the other.

By anticipating the response of the other organism to our gesture we are able, Mead claims, to see ourselves from the perspective of the other. However, in its most elementary stages, role-taking depends on memory images of past social acts. This is not to say that there is an imitative impulse; what Mead emphasizes is the logical need for some prior experiential material before embarking on the first role-taking endeavours. Into our responses to our own conduct, Mead suggests, 'there naturally flows the memory images [sic] of the responses of those about us, the memory images of those responses of others which were in answer to like actions'.[29] This memory imagery explains why social life is a prerequisite for role-taking: without social experience (i.e. without the other), primates could never have learned how to adopt the perspective of the other. It is thus logically untenable to assume an individualist, asocial and rational beginning for natural languages. Once individual organisms come to possess this memory imagery, they are able to begin to express their social impulses first through the conversation of gestures and then by means of conscious communication. The passage from one situation to the next is only possible because some of our gestures allow us to see ourselves as others do: when the social import of these vocal gestures began to be understood by individual organisms, significant language emerged.

Contrary to what some authors suggest,[30] Mead's theory of the origins and development of natural languages does not limit itself to the reconstruction of the most elementary stages of linguistic development. In some of his lectures,[31] Mead discussed at length what he called the 'moods of language', that is, forms of linguistic interaction that are conceived both as stages of social evolution and as phases of the linguistic act. A brief sketch of these 'moods' suffices to show that Mead's analysis does go beyond the study of one- or two-word sentences. Mead's proposed taxonomy includes the following linguistic moods: the imperative, the subjunctive, the optative and, finally, the indicative mood. These moods are intended to describe the several evolutionary stages in the development of natural languages. At the most elementary of these stages, the imperative mood was the predominant form of communication: social relations were, at this point of evolution, coordinated through force and coercion. Then, as the central nervous system developed in human beings, two other moods of language emerged: the subjunctive, associated with deliberation, and the optative, related to decision-making situations. This is not to say, however, that these two moods simply replaced the imperative mood; on the contrary, human beings now came to possess a wider variety of linguistic competencies – instead of only one, they now had several linguistic moods from which to choose in any given situation. Mead's intention is clear. He wishes to complement his account of phylogeny with this taxonomy of the various linguistic evolutionary stages. For instance, self-consciousness emerges only with the subjunctive mood of language for, as Mead explains, the central nervous system 'stands for the ability to present alternatives by introducing a temporal dimension into action. To get the different possibilities into the present situation, one can suggest the other alternatives. Here, then, is deliberation, conversation, an inner forum or council.'[32] The continued practice of such deliberative and rational activities eventually led to the emergence of the indicative, the latest mood of language. Individuals are now able to indicate different courses of action to themselves as well as to the other individuals involved in the same social act. This linguistic mood fits smoothly into Mead's social theory of the self, as we can see from the following passage:

> We must indicate to ourselves not only the object but also the readiness to respond in certain ways to the object, and this indication must be made in the attitude or role of the other individual to whom it is pointed out

or to whom it may be pointed out. If this is not the case it has not the common property which is involved in significance. It is through the ability to be the other at the same time that he is himself that the symbol becomes significant. The common statement of this is that we have in mind what we indicate to another that he shall do. In giving directions, we give the direction to ourselves at the same time that we give it to another.[33]

We are now able to see that, from the perspective of Mead's social psychology, language plays a central role in at least two respects. Firstly, it constitutes his basic principle of human social organization. In other words, language is given the status of a principle around which life in society developed, in the course of general evolution. Mead's conception of society is thus of an inherently symbolic, cooperative undertaking. But, as I have pointed out, language and significant symbols can be scientifically reconstructed only if we conceive of them as products of the interaction between bodily selves. Secondly, language is responsible for the emergence of the human mind. Mead contends that the human mind should be conceptualized as 'phenomena which have arisen and developed out of the process of communication and of social experience generally'.[34] The Cartesian view of the human mind as a purely individual and rational affair is thus rejected in favour of a perspective that sees it as a product of social life, of evolution and of the symbolic exchange of meaningful gestures.

Both these points deserve detailed treatment. In the case of the symbolic nature of human life, it must be said that this insight is one of the reasons why Mead is rightfully given a place in the sociological canon. This is not to say, however, that the reading of Mead's work suggested by symbolic interactionism, the first distinctively American sociological tradition, is without problems. As we shall see, there are compelling reasons to look at Mead's work beyond the symbolic interactionists' interpretative framework. Still, the symbolic nature of Mead's conception of human subjectivity and social interaction as phases of the one and the same process is undeniable. Let us pursue this point further.

For Mead, the structure of the self is reflective. The self reflectively apprehends and communicates with oneself, other selves and physical objects. The human ability to take the role of the other, the behavioural mechanism responsible for reflectivity, depends in turn on the occurrence of vocal gestures, language and significant symbols. The complexity and oral nature of the vocal gestures permitted the evolutionary passage from the unconscious conversation of gestures to a truly symbolic interaction where one individual can anticipate the response of the other and articulate her own response accordingly. Inner life, i.e. the communication of the self with itself, is modelled after Mead's understanding of intersubjective communication: the internal conversation that constitutes reflective thinking cannot be understood except by reference to interpersonal communication. In turn, Mead explains interpersonal communication through the concept of 'role-taking', which draws heavily on the notion of significant symbol. Thus symbolization is a crucial feature of Mead's understanding of human sociality.

Mead's social psychology is an attempt to reconstruct, scientifically, the origins, conditions and functions of human self-reflectivity, an inherently symbolic activity. What characterizes Mead's philosophy is the combination of an evolutionary and naturalistic outlook with a social and symbolic understanding of human experience. Social classes are barely mentioned at all in his writings, solidarity as a societal steering medium has not the deterministic flavour of Durkheim's conception, a systematic theory of macrosocial conflicts and social stratification is also absent – yet Mead's symbolic view of society has exerted tremendous influence over generations of sociologists and other social scientists. Such an influence shows at least one thing: Mead's notion of 'taking the attitude of the other', the conceptual axis around which he erected his theoretical system, is still today a powerful intellectual tool in understanding the symbolic nature of the world we inhabit.

Turning now to the symbolic and communicative nature of the mind, one has to take into account that this was a controversial thesis to hold, even by a social psychologist such as Mead. His thesis that 'having a mind' presupposes symbolic interaction runs counter to a long philosophical tradition which equated reflective thinking with the atomized and abstract individual, from Descartes's reflective cogito to British empiricists like John Locke. Only with Hegel, one of Mead's major sources of inspiration until the mid-1910s, did reflectivity begin to be seen as a social affair. Mead, however, diverged from Hegel as to the solution of the so-called 'blind spot dilemma', which states that the reflective self can reflect on everything else but itself – at least not with satisfactory objectivity. Whereas Hegel suggested the speculative notion of 'absolute reflection' as a means to guarantee complete self-transparent reflectivity, Mead opted instead for a dual conception of the self (closer to Adam Smith's looking-glass metaphor), which we will discuss at length in the next chapter. For now, it suffices to point out that Mead's social theory of the self represents an authentic 'social turn' in Western thought, from the solipsist paradigm inaugurated by Descartes to the intersubjectivist paradigm of which Mead himself is a key figure.

Mead constructs his position on the origins of self-consciousness around the thesis that the mind is an emergent from linguistic interaction. 'Out of language', Mead argues, 'emerges the field of mind'.[35] This assertion, as we have been discussing, was not consensual. Apart from the Cartesian interpretation of the human mind as a substance separate from the physical body, Mead had also to prove his point against Watsonian psychological behaviourism. From this latter perspective, the mind could be accounted for solely in terms of physiology or neurology. Mead plainly rejects such a conventional behaviourist interpretation for its asocial portrait of human experience. Even though he is ready to recognize that physiological developments were essential as the material cause for the emergence of the mind, he nevertheless emphasizes, in a crucial passage from *Mind, Self, and Society*, that

> [t]he evolutionary appearance of mind or intelligence takes place when the whole social process of experience and behavior is brought within the experience of any one of the separate individuals implicated therein . . . It is by means of reflexiveness – the turning-back of experience of the individual upon himself – that the whole social process is thus brought into the experience of the individuals involved in it . . . Reflexiveness, then, is the essential condition, within the social process, for the development of the mind.[36]

Albeit physiologically dependent on the brain, mind can only emerge out of the matrix of social experiences. Each individual organism realizes its physiological potential by participating in social life. Only then will it be able to exercise the human being's distinctive feature of thinking, that is, to behave in a significantly symbolic manner. Since symbolic expression is originally linguistic, there is no mind without language and its content is 'only a development and product of social interaction'.[37] In short, the mind should be confused neither with the brain, nor with some speculative notion of 'pure substance'; for Mead, the mind is an emergent from the social process of human experience.

4

The Social Self

In the previous chapter I have tried to show how Mead can help us to understand why Robinson Crusoe could never have developed a self, had he been abandoned as a newborn child on the island. For Mead, the whole is to be conceived as prior to the part, not the other way round; the individual is to be explained in terms of the society, not the society in terms of the individual. This logical and chronological precedence of the social whole over the individual mind explains why Crusoe could only have developed a self within civilization, yet had no problems in living alone for years on that remote island. Mead's intersubjective model of the self does seem to provide a plausible explanation for the social origins of the mental processes which distinguish us, humans, from other animal forms.

In this chapter I wish to go in considerable depth into Mead's account of the self as a social emergent. Mead's life-long research interest in the nature and logic of the development of human consciousness led him to inquire into mental processes, which include (apart from consciousness itself) concepts like mind and reflective intelligence. Mead's processual view of reality will come here to the fore once again. For Mead, human consciousness includes both subjective states of consciousness (consciousness as 'awareness') and objective functional processes (consciousness as 'reflective intelligence'). Instead of conceiving of consciousness as a substance located somewhere in the human body or as a metaphysical entity, he opts for defining it in terms of its functions and in the light of its social nature. Consciousness, in the sense of reflective intelligence – not to be confused with the subjective conscious states of 'consciousness', understood as awareness – is a functional process taking place in the environment we live in and of which we are a part. Likewise, both reflective intelligence and the mind are understood in terms of a relation between the individual organism and the environment. At one end, this relation involves our ability to cope with the action-problems we face in our dealings with the world, while at the other end it describes that part of our experience – a part to which we have privileged access – in which we discover that we are, individually, objects to ourselves. The mind is not located in the pineal gland, as Descartes wanted it; it is equated with the social process which is the individual's inner conversation to oneself.

The present chapter will proceed from a discussion of the self and of its two developmental stages, 'play' and 'game'. It is important to be aware of Mead's interest in childhood development. He always showed great eagerness to find illustrations for his socio-psychological ideas in children's behaviour. This statement of interest is true both in personal terms (he and his wife were actively engaged in the creation of the Laboratory School at the premises of the University of Chicago, and enrolled their son Henry in it) and in intellectual terms, since, as we shall see, Mead's evolutionary conception of the social self cannot be understood without a reference to the developmental stages of play and game. The inner structure of the self, with its two phases, the 'I' and the 'me', will be the next and final issue to be discussed. I will try to show how Mead conceived of the self as a social process with two aspects and perspectives, different but interrelated: the self internalizes social attitudes as a 'me' and responds to it as an 'I'. While it is the case that one can analytically distinguish between these two phases, the fact remains that the inner structure of the social self can only be understood by reference to the dialectical relation connecting the 'me' and the 'I'. Only by reference to the whole (the self) do the parts (the 'I' and the 'me') attain their meaning. Just one remark before we proceed. Wherever possible, I will illustrate Mead's ideas with concrete examples, very much of the same kind as the ones Mead used in his classes. In this way I hope to render accessible to a wider audience Mead's fascinating insights on the modern self.

Consciousness, reflective intelligence and mind

What is consciousness? How is consciousness connected to our body and our social and cultural life? Is it primarily a biological phenomenon, lodged in some specific organ of the human body, or does it relate to something else, of a more social and interpersonal nature? Consider the example of young Mozart playing the violin at the age of four. He was certainly conscious of the impression he was making upon those who listened to him in awe. But was Mozart's consciousness of that awe around him something located in his brain, or did it emerge from social interaction, that is, from some kind of bond, or connection, with his audience? Mead would have no doubts in answering this question:

precocious Mozart's awareness must have been (like everyone else's) an emergent from social interaction. Of course, awareness and reflective thinking are but different kinds of consciousness, but before I dwell into what distinguishes them I wish to make a further point.

Mead conceives of consciousness not as a substantive phenomenon lodged in the brain, but functionally, as an ongoing process located in the 'objective' world. His declared intention is to avoid the rigid distinction between physical things on one side and mental events on the other. Consciousness is not the precondition of social interaction but its product; consciousness is an emergent of social interaction, not something that was there for conduct to give evidence of. Mead distinguishes between consciousness as 'awareness' and consciousness as involving reflective intelligence. With the former, 'loss of consciousness' refers to situations where we render ourselves inaccessible to the world (e.g. when we go to sleep); with the latter, 'consciousness' is used in connection with our dealings with the social world as reflective intelligent beings. What is at stake here is the distinction between consciousness understood as a subjective experience of objects or feelings to which the individual self alone has access, and self-consciousness, taken to refer to the way we think about the social world or, as Mead puts it, 'to the ability to call out in ourselves a set of definite responses which belong to the others of the group'.[1] Self-consciousness is, then, intimately related to reflective thinking and sociality: it relates to a structure within the self which arises out of social experience and is primarily reflective. Contrary to the subjective conscious states that form 'consciousness' as awareness, 'consciousness' as reflective intelligence is a functional process taking place in the environment we find ourselves in.

Of course, it is not possible to discuss Mead's notion of 'consciousness' without a reference to the concept of 'meaning'. As we have seen, the triadic structure of meaning includes the gesture of the first organism, the responding gesture of the second organism and the 'resultant' of the social act created between them. In other words, Mead rejects equating meaning with a psychical phenomenon of some sort; rather, meaning is implicit in the structure of the social act. Thus meaning neither depends on consciousness for its existence, since it precedes it, nor should be confused with it. Meaning precedes consciousness insofar as it is present in the structure of the social act prior to the emergence of consciousness. This is why an animal can act in a meaningful way without being aware or conscious of that meaning: in any case, for an external rational observer, the meaning of that act can be apprehended with no particular difficulty.

At the very heart of the mental processes lies the notion of 'reflective intelligence'. To begin with, Mead argues that 'reflective behavior arises only under the conditions of self-consciousness'.[2] It is reflection that enables the individual organism to control and adjust its conduct with reference to the surrounding environment. Exactly how does this process of adjustment occur? Imagine that a man is driving on a deserted road and he suddenly runs out of petrol. In order to solve this problem, the man can choose from several alternative courses of action open to him: he could call 999 for the police; try to walk to the nearest petrol station; stay in the car and wait for help – and so on. For Mead, 'intelligence is largely a matter of selectivity':[3] the deliberate choice of one alternative among several is what distinguishes intelligent behaviour from instinctive or habitual conduct. In particular, reflective intelligence is defined by a delayed reaction to a stimulus. Mead distinguishes three different components in this delayed reaction. Firstly, instead of reacting instinctively to the problem of finding petrol, the man has the ability to inhibit action temporarily and to make use of that time in order to review in his mind the courses of action available. Secondly, through his ability to engage in an inner conversation, the man is able to test out mentally the various options available. By comparison with the method of trial and error, this ability to test mentally is much more effective: the man does not actually have to try every alternative course of action, he can simply imagine the pros and cons associated with each. Thirdly, the man is able to choose one out of a set of alternatives rather than simply reacting to the first thing that occurs to him. Intelligence is thus the ability to solve problems we face in the present in terms of our past experience and of our ability to imagine their future consequences. It is this process of exercising intelligence 'which permits the individual's taking of the attitude of the other toward himself, and thus becoming an object to himself. This is the most effective means of adjustment to the social environment . . .'[4]

As suggested in this passage, reflective intelligence and mind are closely related concepts. In particular, 'reflexiveness is the essential condition for the development of the mind'.[5] How does Mead define mind? Far from conflating the mind and the brain, he favours a functional and social definition of mind. Such an approach was at odds with Descartes's rationalistic perspective, which located the mind in a specific part of the human body (the pineal gland). For Mead, by contrast, the mind is the thoroughly social process which consists in 'the importation of the conversation of gestures into the conduct of the individual organism',[6] i.e. an inner conversation. Mead's social theory of mind is more radical than one might think at first glance. He is not suggesting that the mind is a biological entity (an organ of the body) which happens to have social implications – social experience would thus be a consequence of biological factors. On the contrary, Mead argues that mind is a thoroughly social affair, a product of social experience. In a posthumously published paper, he specifies:

> Mind is that part of experience in which the individual becomes an object to himself in the presentation of different lines of conduct. This presentation takes place by means of imagery of past experience whose presence is conditioned by the past experience of the individual and the attitudes which it has left.[7]

According to this definition, mind is neither to be confused with an organ located somewhere in the human body, nor should it be understood as some sort of metaphysical substance (a soul). It is a social phenomenon, which emerges when the individual acquires the ability of pointing out meanings to others and to himself – mind emerges from, and can be understood only by reference to, the empirical world of social interactions. For instance, one says 'to my mind, A is better than B' in order to distinguish one's opinion from other people's views: it is the privileged access an individual has to that part of experience in which she becomes an object to herself that enables her to differentiate her mind from that of the next fellow. What Mead wishes to avoid at all cost is a subjectivistic and idealistic conception of mind – as, for instance, the one put forth by Charles Horton Cooley, whom Mead accuses of solipsism: on that view, society exists only in the individual's mind, and the social conception of the self is but a product of the imagination.[8] In order to avoid such solipsism, Mead argues, it is necessary to endorse a naturalistic and objectivistic social-psychological perspective which conceives of mind as including, and arising from, a matrix of social interactions among individuals.

From this viewpoint, the mind is as much an emergent from social experience as it is a crucially useful resource for solving the problems we face in the empirical world surrounding us. Mind is thus a socially acquired resource whereby the individual organism solves the multiple adjustment problems that must be dealt with so that action can proceed harmoniously. In other words, Mead sees the human mind as the mechanism 'whereby social reconstruction is effected or accomplished'.[9] What does he mean by 'social reconstruction'? As we shall see in detail, for Mead it is the possession of a mind that allows human beings to turn back critically upon the society or social group to which they belong. This critical reflection upon society entails a reorganization or reconstruction of that social structure by the individual mind. Mead then makes two further points. Firstly, there must exist a set of values shared by all the individual minds involved in this social reconstruction; secondly, such a reconstruction tends to assume the character of an intellectual expansion of the moral conventions of the given society. Of course, this process of social reconstruction will eventually lead to changes in the individual mind. In Mead's view, social reconstruction and personality reconstruction are but different phases of the same organic social process.

One last aspect of Mead's treatment of the mind I wish to discuss refers to the way he contrasts the unity of the self from that of the mind. Briefly, while the unity of the mind is related to the interplay of vocal gestures in the form of significant symbols, the unity of the self is a much larger phenomenon. It refers to the fact that the way that each individual self is structured mirrors the way society is organized. In other words, social structure and the unity of the self are closely related processes: for instance, social membership in a plural and diverse society entails a structure of the self that is also pluralistic. It is important to note, however, that irrespective of the degree of social pluralism, the self is always composed of multiple elementary selves. The unity of the self refers to the complex pattern of social relations in which any given individual is implicated. From Mead's point of view, this is a universal feature of the human being; what is historically contingent is the degree to which this relational pattern reflects a more or less pluralistic society.

It should be clear by now why the unity of the mind is a part of, or, as Mead says, 'an abstraction from',[10] the larger unity of the self: the internalization of the conversation of significant gestures which is the mind leaves out many aspects of the pattern of social interactions reflected in the structure of the self. An example will clarify this distinction. Imagine a member of the American Congress: she is a member of a political party and represents a portion of the American electorate. The 'unity of mind' of our congresswoman refers to the organized character of the social and symbolic process by which she is able to become an object to herself. Her 'unity of self', however, is related to the unity of the social organization to which she belongs. This unity mirrors, apart from all other social institutions that make up American society, the unity of the political organizations within which our imaginary congresswoman develops her political activities – her congressional district, the political party she belongs to and the US House of Representatives. As Mead explained to his students in 1927:

> To get selves, people must come back to the logical situations that have arisen in society. We depend on parties to keep our political machine going. We cannot get a response to an issue directly; there is a psychological necessity to work in parties. This unity is that of the group, and we depend upon it without placing it before ourselves. . . . In such processes one has a heightened sense of the self. Failure to remain in a particular group may mean the breakdown of the self. If one is taking advantage of the group, he does not fully belong to the group. But one cannot exist as a self without the universal, the group, that makes the self possible.[11]

Childhood development: the stages of 'play' and 'game'

When we play with a two-year-old child we are able to imagine ourselves in his role, figure out whether he is happy or not, whether he is
in need of anything. The reverse is not true. It might take a few years
until the child acquires the ability to put himself in our shoes. By
passing from one stage to the other, the child will gradually develop
his self. In what follows I wish to discuss Mead's account of the emergence of the self. As we shall soon see, to Mead the self refers to the
ability to take oneself as an object – an ability which can only be
acquired through social experience. Since the self is a social and symbolic process, neither lower animals nor newborn infants have selves.
But the self is also a mental process. And, as in the case of all Mead's
major concepts, he insists that the self should not be located in self-
consciousness but in social experience.

As we have seen, the mechanism responsible for the development
of the self is the ability to 'take the role of the other', Mead's intersubjectivist version of the old philosophical concept of reflectivity. This
turning back of the individual's experience upon itself can only be
achieved indirectly, through one's putting oneself in the position of
others – be they particular individuals or the social group as a whole.
This distinction between taking the role of someone else and taking the
role of the group is not trivial, as we shall see in a moment. The point
I wish to make here is that, in order to have a self, the individual organism has to be able to transcend his or her own standpoint; each one has
to see oneself as the others do. Only by getting outside of oneself,
so to speak, will one be able to examine oneself in an objective, impersonal way.

In the previous chapter we have seen how Mead accounts for the
genesis of the self from the perspective of the history of the human
species. Now I want to examine his explanation of the genesis of the
self through two stages in childhood development. But one should bear
in mind that Mead saw these two accounts, the phylogenetic and the
ontogenetic, as parallel explanations of human development: the same
mechanisms and principles apply. What differs is only the object of
analysis – the human species and the individual, respectively.

The first stage of childhood development is the 'play stage'. At work
here is the principle of 'taking the attitude of the other'. At this stage
children learn to adopt the role of others by playing at being someone
else. This is the simplest form of being another to one's self. As Mead
explains, 'the child is acquiring the roles of those who belong to his
society'.[12] One of his favourite examples is that of children getting
together to 'play Indian'. To Mead, imitation does not explain what

goes on when children play this part. To 'play Indian' means that the child 'has a certain set of stimuli which call out in itself the responses that they would call out in others, and which answer to an Indian'.[13] The child pretends, for instance, that it is saying something as an Indian, then responds as some other character (say, a cowboy). The roles of Indian, or cowboy, cannot be said to be the product of imitation. Children do not limit themselves to imitating the gestures and sounds of Indians; they act as if they were Indians, at least for themselves.

By learning to play at being something other than they are, children begin to acquire a structured self, that is, they learn to become both subject and object. Mead's thesis seems to be particularly appropriate to explain what goes on with the imaginary playmates invented by most of us when we were children. While creating these invisible companions, we carried on discussions with our imaginary playmates, sometimes for hours at a time. To Mead, this exercise is of crucial importance to the development of the capacity to be an object of our own experience. At this stage, though, children only take the attitude of separate, particular individuals and, as such, have only limited selves. For children to acquire a more generalized and organized sense of themselves, i.e. to have a fully developed self, they must get through the 'game stage'. This second stage in childhood development differs from the 'play stage' insofar as the child must now take the role of everyone else involved in the game and coordinate her action accordingly. In play it is possible for children to shift from one role to another as they please: now they play the Indian, now they play the cowboy. In a game, by contrast, the child takes a definite stance, and her actions are defined by reference to the rules of the game. These rules provide the structure within which the limits of each role are determined. Furthermore, the rules of the game constitute a reference point against which individual performance can be evaluated. An illustration of such an organized game is Mead's famous example of baseball:

> The child must not only take the role of the other, as he does in the play, but he must assume the various roles of all the participants in the game, and govern his action accordingly. If he plays first base, it is as the one to whom the ball will be thrown from the field or from the catcher. Their organized reactions to him he has imbedded in his own playing of the different positions, and this organized reaction becomes what I have called the 'generalized other' that accompanies and controls his conduct. And it is this generalized other in his experience which provides him with a self.[14]

Several observations are in order concerning this quotation. Firstly, the type of role-taking Mead mobilizes to explain both these developmental stages presupposes some prior social experience. As we have already seen, in its most elementary stages, role-taking depends on memory images of past social acts. Without some initial social experience, children could never have learned how to adopt the perspective of the other. So, even before starting to play at being someone else, the child has to have some prior experiential material, which supports his first role-taking activities. How could a child start playing at being an Indian if he had never seen one (or, at least, an image of one)? And how could the child play the Indian if she had not already acquired some linguistic skills?

Secondly, at the game stage illustrated above, the behavioural organization usually specified in terms of the rules of the game constitutes the unity required for the self. In other words, the 'unity of the self' (which, as we have seen above, refers to the fact that the structure of the self reflects the structure of the community) results from the child's organization of the attitudes of all those involved in the game. Mead insists that this act creates an 'other' – not a particular other such as the 'Indian', but a 'generalized other', representing the attitude of the entire baseball team, in the example above. Of course, the game stage is but the prelude to social life. In this sense, as the child grows up he will come to interact with the larger social community and will come to encompass and organize a more and more comprehensive 'generalized other'. And the more comprehensive the generalized other is, the more unified the self becomes.

Thirdly, this notion of a 'generalized other', one of Mead's most widely known concepts (which be the object of a detailed analysis in the next chapter), is closely related to abstract thinking and objectivity. Mead expands on this idea in 'The Genesis of the Self and Social Control', which some consider to be his most important single philosophical paper.[15] Since thinking is conceived as an inner conversation in which we take the roles of others against ourselves, Mead suggests that 'usually it is with what I have termed the "generalized other" that we converse, and so attain to the levels of abstract thinking, and that impersonality, that so-called objectivity that we cherish'.[16] The attitude of the 'generalized other' is the result of an enlarged self-consciousness, an attitude which expresses better than any other the ideas of objectivity, impersonality and generality. The more comprehensive the generalized other whose role we take, the more objective and abstract our viewpoint will be. However, one should not make the mistake of inferring from this that there is such a thing as an overarching and all-powerful society determining, through the attitude of the generalized other, the individual conduct of the particular selves. For Mead, each social group involves a specific generalized other whose attitude we may take as we engage in social life: in other words, there are as many generalized others in society as there are social groups. Therefore, a coherent and fully developed self takes the attitude of multiple generalized others in an unrepeatable fashion. Each self articulates in a unique way the shared set of social and cultural values. Thus, for Mead, there is no contradiction between a growing tendency towards individuality and an increasing trend towards universalism.

The structure of the self: the I–me distinction

One of the most fascinating ingredients of Mead's thought is his conception of the internal structure of the self. Even though not totally original,[17] Mead's definition of the self as an ongoing social process with two distinguishable phases, the 'I' and the 'me', is nevertheless a distinctive feature of his social psychology. An example may help to clarify the I–me distinction. Imagine a situation in which someone is remembering what he said a few minutes ago. The phase of the self which remembers is the 'I', the phase of the self which is remembered is the 'me'. When the man in our example remembers what he said, in the very act of remembering, the subject of self-reflection (the 'I') is always slipping into the past, leaving only the 'me' as an object of observation. The 'I' disappears at the very moment when it performs its function; once it presents itself as a past actor, it ceases to be an 'I' and becomes a 'me'. There is a permanent process of conversion of the 'I' into a 'me': the person's uncertain activity of responding is continuously being objectified – in retrospect, and through the reactions of the others. Therefore the 'I' is a source of novelty in oneself that may surprise even the self in question: the 'I' is as unknown to the others as it is to its bearer. As should be clear by now, the 'I' and the 'me' are not things, but processes within the larger process that is the self. A person has access to her 'I' only through recollections of her past actions, as a 'historical figure'.

With the above-mentioned example in mind, let us suppose that the individual now engages in a conversation with a group of friends. He does not know what he is going to say in response to the others' remarks, nor does anybody else. The 'I' is that phase of the self through which one responds to the present social situation on the basis of one's own experience; but one's response contains a novel and immediate element. In this sense, the 'I' represents one's assertion of one's own creativity and distinctiveness: it is the uncertain, unpredictable and immediate response of an individual to others. From the perspective of the mechanism of taking the role of the other, the uncertainty associated with the 'I' has considerable consequences. Role-taking entails an element of prediction, since we see ourselves through the 'I' of the other: we have no choice but to try to guess how our interlocutor's 'I' will respond to our action. But there is always an uncertainty about the way others will respond to our actions. This is true even of the simplest social interactions: what one does is always somewhat different from anything we could anticipate.

I would now like to discuss some of the functions performed by the concept of 'I' in Mead's system of thinking, starting with the 'I' as a source of social change. The examples Mead has in mind are those of great figures that have changed the course of history. In his view, 'leaders' or 'geniuses' such as Jesus, Buddha or Socrates have, as social agents, made their communities larger and richer by responding to them in an unusually powerful way. In other words, their 'Is' were singularly strong:

> it is this uniqueness and originality of his response to a given social situation or problem or project – which nevertheless conditions his behavior no less than that of the ordinary individual – that distinguishes the genius from the ordinary individual.[18]

Of course, the functions performed by the 'I' are not limited to what great historical figures did. The 'I' is also held to be responsible for innovative or progressive values. Whereas the values associated with the 'me' tend 'to call out the sacrifice of the self for the whole',[19] the values which attach particularly to the 'I' tend to involve the reconstruction of the social order. To illustrate this sort of value, Mead indicates the attitude of contemporary artists. In their case, 'the emphasis upon the element of novelty is carried to the limit'.[20] In macro-sociological terms, Mead explains the societal tendency for increasing individualism and autonomy by means of the innovative character of the 'I'. In Mead's view, there is a growing proportion of individuals in contemporary societies whose personalities show a stronger component of 'I'. As in the case of great historical figures, ordinary individuals in everyday routine situations can promote social change by giving expression to their 'Is'. As Mead puts it, '[t]o the degree that we make the community in which we live different we all have what is essential to genius'.[21] Mead's democratic and anti-elitist inclinations could not be made any clearer than this.

The 'I' is thus intimately related to critical moral thinking. Distinguishing conventional morality, i.e. the customary and uncritical application of moral norms, from critical moral thinking, in which a reflective examination of the moral problem at hand is pursued, Mead suggests that the response of the 'I' to a situation performs the crucial function of self-assertion: 'One now asserts himself against a certain situation, and the emphasis is on the response'.[22] Through the response of the 'I' we gain a critical distance from conventions, we free ourselves from customs and given laws. There is an appeal to a larger moral community, in which rights are not as restricted as in the existing community. Such an appeal is the attitude of the impulsive and unpredictable 'I' against the conventional 'me'. As we shall see in the next chapter, when we discuss Mead's communicative ethics, Mead's line of argument proceeds with two important suggestions. Firstly, it is by taking the role of the 'generalized other' that individuals are able to sense the larger moral order (which is implied in the set of common attitudes one internalizes when taking that role); secondly, and contrary to what one might think in view of the role performed by the impulsive 'I', Mead suggests that the appeal to a larger, ideal community is a rational affair: 'The rational solution of the conflicts, however, calls for the reconstruction of both habits and values, and this involves transcending the order of the community'.[23]

Turning now to the 'me', one should start by emphasizing that this phase of the self corresponds to the object-self rather than to the subject-I. The 'me' is thus the social object which is to be reconstructed by the 'I'. Within the self, the 'me' relates to our self-image when we look at ourselves through the eyes of the others. When we do that, Mead claims, we import into our conduct the attitudes of the others; therefore, while the 'me' is associated with the way we organize these social attitudes, the 'I' is our impulsive response to them. Contrary to the uncertain nature of the 'I', the 'me' is of a conscious nature. Whereas the impulsive response of the 'I' is unknown both to the others and to its bearer, the 'me' refers to an organized set of social attitudes that one assumes in a conscious way. The individual is aware of the social expectations of the community in which he lives. Mead makes this point in relation to two distinct settings. The organized games children play give them an opportunity to learn how to internalize the organized set of attitudes or responses that stands for the group; later in life, in the context of social institutions such as the family, individuals use this experiential knowledge to realize themselves by recognizing the other in his or her relationship to them. Either playing a game as children or participating in social life as adults, we are able to monitor our own conduct due to the 'me'. Mead writes: 'To have self-consciousness one must have the attitude of the other in one's own organism as controlling the thing that he is going to do. What appears in the immediate experience of one's self in taking that attitude is what we term "me"'.[24]

We see ourselves – our actions and thoughts – from the perspective of others: this is what Mead wishes to emphasize by distinguishing the 'me' as a phase of the self. Of course, it is one thing to understand our conduct from the perspective of an individual other, and another to interpret it from the more general and abstract perspective of a group. In this latter case, as we shall see in the following chapter, one takes the role of the 'generalized other', i.e. one internalizes the abstract perspective of the community.

When we see ourselves from the perspective of either an individual other or a 'generalized other', the self assumes the status of an object to itself. In either case, there is always an agent of reconstruction and an object: the 'me' is that phase of the self when it functions as an object, while the 'I' refers to the self as the principle of action. As we have seen above, the unity of the self reflects the unity of the social group to which one belongs. Since the 'me' is our self-image from the perspective of the others, it is not difficult to see why the unity of the 'me' and the unity of the self are closely related: it is through the 'me', i.e. through the self as an object, that the unity of the social organization is reflected upon the structure of the self.

While the 'I' is conceived of as the source of innovative values and self-realization, the 'me' is associated with the 'conventional, habitual individual'.[25] This conventional individual is a social actor who has the same habits and attitude as everyone else. His ideas can hardly be distinguished from those of his neighbour. Of course, we should keep it in mind that the 'me' is but a phase of the self: in this sense, the conformity to social expectations expressed by the 'me' is perennially in conflict with the spontaneity of the 'I'. Each concrete individual shows, according to Mead, a particular combination of these two elements, in some cases with a greater proportion of the component 'me', sometimes with a greater proportion of the component 'I'. All in all, though, Mead believes that in modern developed societies an increasing number of people have personalities with a greater proportion of 'I'.

To summarize our discussion of the I–me distinction, I would like my readers to pay attention to the following points. Firstly, the 'I' and the 'me' are not things or substances that we can distinguish as we distinguish our hand from our foot; rather, the 'I' and the 'me' are different aspects of the social process called 'the self'. At certain moments, the self can best be described as an 'I', at others as a 'me'. But, I repeat, although they can be distinguished analytically, the 'I' and the 'me' are but different phases of the same (social) process – which is, in turn, only a phase of the even larger process of social life. Secondly, this conception of the I–me distinction, derives from Mead's rejection of the Cartesian separation of the self and the surrounding world. The self is not opposed to the world; rather, it is a part of it. Thus, when someone takes the role of another and obtains a self-image as a result, that person is before a presentation of oneself from the perspective of the other. Mead's radically social conception of the self, however, must not be confused with individually oriented psychological theories. In other words, Mead is not claiming that there is a subjective self that sees itself as the others do, as if there were two discrete levels of perception – the subjective inner life of the self and the objective existence of the world of things. On the contrary, Mead argues that the 'I', in its dialectical relationship with the 'me', is a response, by the individual, to a 'social situation which is within the experience of the individual'.

By bringing social attitudes inside the structure of the self, Mead performs nothing short of a Copernican revolution. The paradigm inaugurated by Descartes determined the strict separation between the self as a thinking entity and the outside world of experience. Mead, articulating the pragmatist processual view of reality with a radically social conception of the self, suggests that the opposite is true. He argues not only that the self and the world are inseparable parts of the same process, but also that the Cartesian rationalistic 'thinking thing' is an illusion: both logically and historically, the emergence and development of the self are intrinsic aspects of the social world that surrounds it.

Let us now proceed with our analysis of Mead's key ideas by focusing on two different problem-areas: on the one hand, the sociological, moral and political aspects of his thinking and, on the other hand, Mead's theory of the act and his concept of 'object'. Though quite distinct, these two dimensions of Mead's work complement, and are closely associated with, his social-psychological theory. My aim in the chapter that follows is to bring to the fore the systematic relations which connect these research areas.

5

Society, Mind and Self

We have so far covered most of Mead's key psychological ideas, from his notion of 'taking the attitude of the other' to his conception of the self as a social emergent. In this chapter, I dwell on two different aspects of Mead's work, which will be shown not only to be closely related but also to throw additional light upon his social psychology. The first of these aspects refers to the sociological implications of Mead's social psychology: his notion of social control, his treatment of institutions and his moral and political thinking will be discussed from the vantage point of Mead's process philosophy. My aim is to call my readers' attention to a part of Mead's work that is usually not given as much attention as his celebrated social psychology. The other aspect I shall discuss is related to Mead's work in the last decade of his career. Partly as a consequence of his disillusionment with institutional politics after World War I, Mead's intellectual production on politics and morals suffered a slight decrease during the 1920s. However, his writings on a four-phased theory of action, on the theory of perception of the physical object that stems from it, and on his theory of time became more numerous and eventually came to assume a central position in his later thought. It is to these issues, particularly his theory of the act and his notion of 'object', that the second part of this chapter is devoted.

Mead and the war: the I–me fusion

The last chapter ended with a discussion of the 'I–me' distinction, the two phases of the self. I now wish to examine this dyad from another perspective. In my view, one of the most important features of the 'I–me' distinction is that, on certain occasions, these two phases of the self can lose their distinctive character and merge. This process of fusion between the 'I' and the 'me' occurs when 'the reaction which one calls out in others is the response which one is making himself',[1] such as in situations of intense religious or patriotic fervour. A concrete application of this idea can be found in the 1915 article 'The Psychological Bases of Internationalism'.

In that article Mead starts his analysis of the war in Europe by taking note of its 'great spiritual dividends'.[2] Arguing along similar lines to those of Simmel and Durkheim,[3] Mead asserts that individual members of societies can fuse into self-conscious nations in moments of exceptional emotional intensity. Like tides of national consciousness that sweep across the body of citizenry, these emotional moments are as intense as they are brief. When such moments occur, Mead contends that there is a fusion between the 'I' and the 'me': in other words, there is an absolute identification between the individual self and the social group. The fusion of the individual and the group is so complete that the individual can even lose himself 'in the whole group in some sense, and may attain the attitude in which he undergoes suffering and death for the common cause'.[4] When this happens, when individual existence is sacrificed for the sake of the community, social fusion is complete and absolute.

Mead, however, is far from endorsing the irrationalist implications suggested by this psychological phenomenon. On the contrary, his proposed solution for settling international disputes comprises two elements drawn from his scientific social psychology. Firstly, rejecting James' assumption of a masculine fighting instinct, Mead asks why reformist activities should be seen as 'white-blooded'; at any rate they are a 'vastly more intelligently conceived' formulation of the same patriotic principles.[5] In Mead's view, social reform is intrinsically internationalist since it gives priority to the interests of humankind over those of the state. Secondly, both in the notion of self-reflectivity as the elemental mechanism for the development of the self and in the idea of democratic self-rule, understood as the basic condition for a meaningful group life, the same insight is suggested. As Mead observes: 'The function of social organization is to build up and enlarge the personality of nations as truly as that of individuals, and this cannot include the deliberate destruction of the very members of international society, the consciousness of whom is essential to national self-consciousness.'[6]

Just as an individual depends on the existence of other human beings in order to exist himself, so the national identity and the very life of a political community is dependent on the existence of other nation-states. This is why Mead concludes this essay by stating that the solution for the problem of militarism, the chief cause of conflict, is of a psychological nature. It lies in a change of attitude on the part of the states of the Central Powers, which would indicate 'the willingness to accept the whole international fabric of society, and to regard the states and the communities of which they are the instruments, as subject to and controlled by the life of the whole, not as potential enemies for whose assault each state must be forever on the watch'.[7] According to Mead, then, as long as the state apparatus is conceived of as a mechanism through which the political community may undertake its deliberate corporate actions, it will incorporate the values of society itself; political institutions are but instruments of the collective will, which have incorporated the principle of revolution and transformed it into a constitutional imperative for gradual change.

The horrors of warfare did not diminish Mead's confidence in reason as the most effective way of conflict resolution. One has to keep in mind the fact that Mead thinks of reason as a social construction: 'human intelligence', he explains, evolved in the history of the human species through successive stages as the result of linguistic intercourse between fellow humans. Science, from Mead's perspective, is but the most advanced stage in the evolution of human rationality. The resistance to rational resolution exhibited in moral and political affairs not only can be explained by scientific means, but must be superseded through a scientific approach to morals and politics. This is why Mead, in the latter part of the 1920s – a decade he dedicated almost entirely to epistemology and the philosophy of science – reiterated most of his earlier political theses.

A case in point is his 'National-Mindedness and International-Mindedness' (1929), a paper in which Mead returns to his earlier account of the 'hostile impulse' in order to describe the social-psychological instinct responsible for 'the spiritual exaltation of wartime patriotism'.[8] Against this instinctive feeling, Mead opposes 'the power which language has conferred upon us, of not only seeing ourselves as others see us but also of addressing ourselves in terms of the common ideas and functions which an organized society makes possible'.[9] Retaining the evolutionary perspective which characterizes his theory of phylogenesis, Mead argues that nationalism is a historically recent phenomenon, whereby men suddenly realized that they belonged to communities transcending their families and clans. In this sense, 'national-mindedness' is to be conceived of as a conversation with a 'generalized other', more general than previous forms of human association but less general than the form idealized by Mead. As he puts it: 'Can we carry on a conversation in international terms?'[10] According to him, the 'moral equivalent of war', to paraphrase James, is to be found in the socially acquired capacity for the rational linguistic expression of ideas, rather than in some fundamental social impulse. It is a cognitivist and internationalist solution that Mead proposes. Social conflicts, ranging from labour disputes or educational issues to armed conflicts, are to be solved according to the principles of the method of modern science and the teachings of social psychology. In the case of warfare, what is needed is the institutionalization of the problem-solving attitude that characterizes the scientist. In this sense, the League of Nations, whose creation on 28 June 1919 (with the signing of the Treaty of Versailles) was enthusiastically endorsed by Mead, is the political institution whose function it is to determine the common interests that lie behind every conflict of interests. In Mead's words, the 'moral equivalent of war is found in the intelligence and the will both to discover these common interests between contending nations and to make them the basis for the solution of the existing differences and for the common life which they will make possible'.[11]

The 'me', the 'generalized other' and social control

One further aspect related to the 'me' which I would like to draw upon consists in its connection with the notion of the 'generalized other'. The 'me' is, in a sense, the representative of the community within the self. This importation of social attitudes into the self is performed through the 'generalized other'. It is by taking the role of the 'generalized other' that we can see ourselves from the perspective of all the members of the group. As we have seen above, the game stage yields the concept of the 'generalized other'. During that developmental stage, children learn how to look at themselves from the perspective of everyone else. The attitude of the 'generalized other' is a concept used by Mead to describe the social attitudes of the organized community, as the individual internalizes them by means of his 'me'. In fact, the 'me' emerges when children begin to take the role of the 'generalized other'. When a child learns to see himself from the perspective of all his team-mates, his personality begins to exhibit a unity and structure which reflect the unity and structure of the social group. Hence, the 'generalized other' is a crucial element in the development of a full grown personality:

> only in so far as he takes the attitudes of the organized social group to which he belongs toward the organized, co-operative social activity or set of such activities in which that group as such is engaged, does he develop a complete self.[12]

This is one of Mead's most innovative insights. Social rules, Mead suggests, are not simply transmitted to a passive individual self. On the contrary, Mead's 'generalized other' points to a totally different way in which social attitudes become incorporated into the self. Far from being a passive recipient of social rules, Mead's self is an active interpreter of the group's attitudes: 'The self, as such, is a rational entity and always involves talking to oneself in terms of the group, the generalized other'.[13] The underlying picture of the relation between the individual self and the social group is clear. For Mead, we are able to participate in the life of the community (from the simplest childhood game to the most demanding moral judgement or scientific reasoning), not because we play pre-given social roles, but because we interpret and reformulate in our mind the attitudes that are common to the group.[14]

The moral and political implications of Mead's concept of 'taking the attitude of the generalized other' are not difficult to discern. It is by talking to ourselves in terms of the group that we become able to sense the larger moral order, which is implicit in the common attitudes associated with the 'generalized other'. Mead's approach to morality is founded upon a clear political agenda. Distinguishing between conventional and critical moral thinking, Mead equates the latter with the qualities of rationality, impartiality and self-criticism. Social actors can assume a critical moral stance towards a given ethical problem by taking the role of the generalized other. To act rationally is to act in a self-critical manner, and self-criticism is but a form of social criticism. What is more, social control and self-criticism are also closely related phenomena. Let us explore this important insight a little further.

The fact that the 'me' involves the adoption of the attitude of the 'generalized other' entails one important consequence: it is through the 'me' that social control is exerted upon the individual. In other words, society exercises control over the conduct of its members in the form of the 'generalized other', who is internalized in individual personalities through the 'me'. This internalization takes place by means of the ability to adopt someone else's role; moreover, as Mead observes, the 'immediate effect of such rôle-taking lies in the control which the individual is able to exercise over his own response'.[15] Concomitantly, when the individual assumes the attitude of the 'generalized other', society can exert a certain degree of control over his or her conduct. Still, it must be said that Mead's notion of social control does not contain any overwhelming pressure from the external community upon the inner consciousness of individuals. In fact Mead contends that social control, 'far from tending to crush out the human individual or to obliterate . . . individuality, is, on the contrary, actually constitutive of and inextricably associated with that individuality'.[16] The social nature of the self is not incompatible with every individual having a peculiar and singular biography. Individuality is, in Mead's view, the flipside of universalism. The more universal the values of our community of reference, the more space there is for individuality. The reason for this lies in the fact that the personality structure of each self reflects the organized structure of society as a whole; however, it does so from its own particular and unique standpoint within that process, and thus reflects in its organized structure a different aspect or perspective of this whole social behavior pattern from that which is reflected in the organized structure of any other individual self within that process.[17]

Social control should, in effect, be equated with self-criticism. Individuals become self-conscious when they adopt the attitudes of other individuals towards them, in particular the attitude of the 'generalized other'. They are then able to monitor and control their own conduct by reference to social conventions and expectations. Such a self-critical attitude is performed by means of the 'me' – which explains why self-criticism is in fact social criticism. For Mead, there is no inner subjectivity on the one hand, external social life on the other. Self-consciousness is a thoroughly social affair and social life is essentially a process of symbolic exchange. It is as members of society, as participants in the life of the community, that we are continuously defining who we are. A person's assertion of her distinctiveness and her conformity to social rules are to be seen as two interrelated and mutually constitutive phases of one single dialectical process – not as two separate dimensions.

Society, ethics and democracy

Even though Mead's most influential insights are not related to large-scale social and political processes, his analysis of society, institutions, ethics and democratic politics can still be illuminating. To use a metaphor suggested by Quentin Skinner's work, the macro-components of Mead's philosophy may not form the bulk of his intellectual treasure, but a historical examination of them can certainly help us to establish a critical distance from our own beliefs.[18] Let us begin with Mead's conception of society.

As I have already suggested, the order of the terms in Mead's book-title, *Mind, Self, and Society*, does not reflect the internal logic of his analysis. To describe the order in which Mead conceives of those elements, the title should have been 'Society, self, and mind'. In other words, society precedes the mind and the self both logically and temporally. From this point of view, Mead gives society a central explanatory role in his social-psychological theories.

From a related perspective, Mead sees society as being internalized by the individual self in the form of the 'me'. Here society is conceived of as the 'organized set of responses' individuals can use for purposes of social control – which, as we have seen, operates in terms of self-criticism. And there is yet another viewpoint from which Mead addresses the concept of society: society as a modern industrial formation – the concrete society he lived in. In 'The Genesis of the Self and

Social Control' (1925), Mead sets himself the question whether, given the increasing complexity of modern industrial societies, the 'modern' person can, better than their predecessors, put themselves in the place of those who contribute to their needs or share their civic duties. The societal shift towards modernity, with its associated processes of urbanization and industrialization, does not seem to affect Mead's faith in human progress achieved through the application of human intelligence to the resolution of social problems. For he writes:

> As long as the complexities of human society do not exceed those of the central nervous system, the problem of an adequate social object, which is identical with that of an adequate self-consciousness, is not that of becoming acquainted with the indefinite number of acts that are involved in social behavior, but that of so overcoming the distances in space and time, and the barriers of language anti convention and social status, that we can converse with ourselves in the roles of those who are involved with us in the common undertaking of life.[19]

Dying as he did in 1931, Mead's confidence in modernity – or that of his contemporary pragmatist colleagues, for that matter – would never be shaken by the horrors of Auschwitz and the possibility of the self-annihilation of the species through a nuclear Armageddon. This is not to say, however, that Mead's conception of science amounted to some sort of naive positivism applied to the social and human sciences. I wish to emphasize that Mead's account of modernity is much less sceptical and pessimistic than the accounts one finds in Marx, Nietzsche, Freud or Weber. An instance that seems to confirm this thesis of mine can be found in Mead's conception of 'institution'.

To Mead, the general process of social differentiation has two poles. On the one hand, he points to social impulses as the physiological basis upon which social interactions take place. On the other hand, there is the institutional pole, 'constituted by the responses of individuals to the identical responses of others, that is, to class or social responses'.[20] Institutions, from Mead's perspective, are defined in terms of socially common responses. Under certain circumstances, the social group acts towards the individual in an identical way: it is then that an institution is formed. For example, if everyone responds in the same manner to someone claiming a house as his property (let us say that they respect his claim), then one can speak of the institution of 'property'. An institution is thus a social process insofar as it depends on the internalization, by people, of a set of organized attitudes. It is by taking the attitude of the 'generalized other' that individual selves become 'institutionalized individuals'. Of course, the way the 'I' of each individual will respond to this internalization by the 'me' varies according to the particular character of each self. So, for instance, the common response of the community when someone asserts their property rights over a house varies according to the character of the person in question: for example, the response of a thief will certainly be different from the response of a police officer or a neighbour.

Operating with this definition, Mead does not see any reason why social institutions should be necessarily oppressive. On the contrary, many social institutions are actually 'flexible and progressive, fostering individuality rather than discouraging it'; and he then points out that, in any case, 'without social institutions of some sort . . . there could be no fully mature individual selves or personalities at all'.[21] Far from endorsing a fatalistic and determinist conception of institutions as socially organized means of control over individual creativity, Mead argues that they need only to define people's lines of conduct in a very broad and general sense, and they should afford a wide scope for originality and self-expression. In his view, social institutions can both constrain and enable one's assertion of one's own distinctiveness. What actually happens is a matter of historical contingency, not the result of some 'iron law'.

Turning now to Mead's approach to ethics, one should begin by noting that his communicative ethics aims at defining general principles of moral problem-solving. As such, Mead's proposal is proceduralist rather than teleological. It focuses not so much on the definition of a determined final end supposed to motivate moral action as on the definition of procedures in a democratic and experimental moral method.

The method of ethics is explicitly defined by reference to the procedures of the experimental scientific method. According to Mead, the resolution of a moral problem requires, much as a scientific problem does, that 'all of the interests that are involved should be taken into account. One should act with reference to all of the interests that are involved: that is what we could call a "categorical imperative".'[22] The resolution of moral problems is inspired by the example of the research scientist in that both the critical moral agent and the scientist have to take into consideration all the relevant facts. Since moral problems involve conflicts between opposing ends, the crux of the question is the ability to keep the wider perspective in mind. Only in this way can all of the points of view in conflict be fully appreciated. Thus one can see that Mead's ethics is of a communicative nature, since the problem of bearing in mind all the perspectives is ultimately a problem of communication: each and every side in conflict must be able to express their viewpoints in a manner that is intelligible to all the others. Hence, Mead's theory of ethics is universalistic insofar as it is oriented to the rational perspective of the 'generalized other' and, in particular, to the 'rational community that is represented in the so-called universe of discourse'.[23]

For me, the clearest instance of Mead's attempt to provide a scientific basis for his moral theory is the 1923 article 'Scientific Method and the Moral Sciences'. Adducing various examples of concrete applications of his proposed theory, ranging from public health to municipal politics and nationalism, Mead argues that both the ethical ends and the means to attain them are 'subject to restatement and reconstruction' by the 'intelligent method of science'.[24] And he goes on to suggest that there is an internal connection between the experimental method of modern science and democratic politics. Both in a research laboratory and in a parliament, the human ability to communicate in a rational fashion is the basis upon which the coordination of the conduct of individuals, either as scientists or as citizens, is carried out. From this perspective, it is only natural that Mead raises serious doubts about the purely quantitative aspects of democratic life. Much more important than the 'clumsy method of registering public sentiment which the ballot box affords in a democracy'[25] are – to Mead as to Dewey[26] – the continued and informed debates within a cognitively competent and civically engaged citizenry. The radical democratic implication of Mead's communicative ethics is that scientific knowledge should be disseminated throughout all social layers, so that every individual citizen can have access, by means of his or her intelligence, to the results of science. The rational communicative basis of Mead's democratic ideal is clear. All social and political institutions should be permeable to a communication flowing from an informed citizenry; the necessary and sufficient condition for this to happen is the definition of the rational procedure for attaining agreements through mutual understanding. Science and democracy, sustained by universal education and intelligent social reform, are, in a clear pragmatist fashion, the sources of inspiration for Mead's proposed solutions to the problems of modern industrial society.

Let me pick up again the idea that reversing the order of items in Mead's title *Mind, Self, and Society* would express his point of view concerning the precedence of society over minds and selves. But even more important than getting the order of those elements right is to realize the organic and functional nature of Mead's conception of the relationship between the individual self and society. It has to be emphasized that Mead does not see the self as a substance, with a varying proportion of unconscious and conscious components, but as a process. The self is, from his perspective, a social process with two distinguishable phases, the 'I' and the 'me'. Just as, for Dewey, 'stimulus' and 'response' constitute distinct moments in conduct, so too, for Mead, the 'I' and the 'me' are functional categories rather than 'things'. Moreover, Mead asserts that the self is but a 'phase of the whole social organization of which the individual is a part'.[27] The self is a phase in the general ongoing process which constitutes society, insofar as it is able to import into its own conduct the organized set of attitudes of the community. As a result, the social order gains an increased coordination as individuals become more efficient members of society. This insight – that we are continually affecting the society in we live in and, in turn, being continually moulded by it – is at the very heart of Mead's understanding of social life as a symbolic exchange. Significant symbols and reflective intelligence form what distinguishes human beings from all other living forms on earth: Mead's most innovative and relevant contribution lies precisely in working out the origins, process of development and implications of the symbolic nature of our world. This is *our* world in an important sense, namely because we create it.

The theory of the act

One of the most innovative elements of Mead's social psychology is his four-phased model of action – the 'theory of the act'. Briefly, at stake here is an analysis of the various temporal dimensions of human conduct: Mead conceives of every human act as a dynamic whole composed of several successive stages. As he explains in *The Philosophy of the Act* (1938), an 'act' describes the relation between organism and environment, an 'ongoing event that consists of stimulation and response and the results of the response'.[28] As such, an act should be seen as an organic whole, something which unfolds in a number of phases; these can be separated through analysis but cannot be understood except by reference to the whole act.

As I have already said, Mead conceives of the act as consisting of four stages. The first one of them is the impulse to action. At the beginning of any act there is a physiological predisposition of the organism to respond to a given stimulus. Perception is the next phase. At this second stage, the organism perceives either an object or a part of the surrounding environment. The third phase of an action is manipulation. The organism, after perceiving a distant object, will move either towards or away from it. In most cases, the perceptual phase of the act leads to the manipulation of the object, either physically (as in the case, say, of an apple) or intellectually (as in the case of a past event).[29] As Mead emphasizes, manipulation is a very important phase in human conduct, for it provides the experience of contact which enables us to see 'things hard or soft, rough or smooth, big or little in measurement with ourselves, hot or cold and wet or dry. It is this imaged contact that makes the seen thing an actual thing.'[30] Mead considers perception and manipulation to be the intermediate phases of the ongoing act; the fourth and final phase occurs when the organism attributes a certain value to the object in question, thereby consummating the act. Consummation, therefore, completes the act.

This temporal analysis of the various phases of the act should be enough to make us see that Mead's conception of human action excludes one-sided explanations: action is not to be understood either as a purely individualistic affair, or as being totally determined by external factors (social, cultural or economic). Instead, the originally social beginning of human interaction leads to increasingly higher levels of individuality both in the history of the species and in the history of each human being.

By conceiving of the 'act' as a gesture of a bodily organism (which is a physical thing) in relation to the surrounding environment, Mead wishes to combine a naturalistic explanation of human perception (a well-known pragmatist theme) with the insight that rational individuals owe their rationality and individuality to the social experience in which they take part and of which they are products: reflective consciousness is not a given. Social interaction between individual organisms is the precondition for the development of human beings, whose individuality, in turn, will increase only through social experience (albeit now of a more complex nature, namely of a linguistic character).[31] Consider Mead's notion of 'object'. For him, what distinguishes the human self is the ability to be 'an object to himself'.[32] Indeed, Mead goes as far as to argue that this 'self-objectifying' attitude is closely related to human rationality: one is rational to the extent to which one is able to take an impersonal, objective attitude towards oneself.

According to Mead, the ability to perceive objects is not innate, but learned through interaction with the surrounding environment in so-called problem-situations. How, then, does the individual organism come to perceive itself as one object among others? First of all, Mead distinguishes between physical and social objects. His proposed distinction is closely related to his four-phased theory of the act, and is based upon the thesis that we form social objects before we form physical objects: the social consciousness precedes the consciousness of physical objects. At first, human organisms interact socially with the surrounding environment and the objects it is composed of. The immediate response of an organism towards an inanimate physical object is the same as its response towards another organism. For instance, I love the pen I usually work with and I hate my mobile phone when its battery runs out.[33] But after a while, individuals 'abstract from that type of response because of what we come to know of such objects'.[34] There are, then, two different moments when we deal with physical objects: our immediate response is social, while our later reaction is abstract and rational. What explains the passage from one moment to the other is the human hand. In a sense, physical things are the product of the human hand. By perceiving and manipulating things we respond to them as physical objects, surpassing the initial immediate social response, but this happens still before we consummate the act. As perception and manipulation are the intermediate phases of the act, so the physical objects (created by the human hand) come 'betwixt and between the beginning of the act and its consummation'.[35] In the case of my pen, when I write with it the pen becomes a physical object, with a certain weight, colour and other qualities; when I finish writing a sentence, I can think back and realize how much my handwriting owes to my favourite pen. Mead makes a further point. He argues that the pen, as a physical thing, is a universal in the sense of belonging to the experience of everyone holding a pen, notwithstanding the fact that the consummation of the act has an inescapably particular character.

Referring back to my earlier point that Mead's ethical thinking is closely related to his theory of the act, one should note that his intention is to found an ethical theory upon his 'social theory of the origin, development, nature, and structure of the self'.[36] In other words, Mead wishes to provide an ethics which is sensitive to the social nature of the individual – one where, for instance, the universal character of ethical judgements lies only in their sociality. I would like to underline two points. The first is the fundamental analogy Mead draws between the method of ethics and scientific procedure; the second is the location of the value of an object in the phase of the consummation of the act.

It is from the point of view of the 'bodily organism as a physical thing' in relation to the surrounding environment that Mead addresses the issue of the value of an object.[37] According to his theory of action, one can observe a specific kind of relation between subject and object in each of the various phases of the act. During the phase of perception from a distance, the subject can establish a cognitive relation with the 'secondary qualities' of the object, such as its colour or sound. However, the highest objectivity can only be attained at the next phase – that of manipulation: it is then that the 'primary qualities' of the object (such as mass) are apprehended by the subject. Finally, during the phase of consummation the subject is able to evaluate the object, even if his judgement at this point is more vulnerable to cultural or historical factors, diminishing its objectivity.[38] These being the foundations upon which Mead constructs his ethical theory, one will understand why in this ethics values can be the object of rational examination even if Mead rejects both an objectivist and a subjectivist conception of value. The value of an object arises in the context of the relation between subject and object, being neither an objectively given thing nor a subjective mental affair.

We are now able to summarize our examination of Mead's key social-psychological ideas. I would like to emphasize three main ideas, which correspond approximately to the issues discussed in chapters 3 to 5. Firstly, Mead's greatest contribution lies in having provided a sustained alternative to Descartes's rationalism. Mead's conception of the self as an emergent from social experience provides a cogent alternative to Cartesian atomism, without making the opposite mistake of reducing human experience to its sociological aspects. The intersubjective character of Mead's theory comes to the fore with the crucial notion of taking the role or attitude of the other. This concept allows Mead to readdress the old philosophical theme of reflectivity in an innovative way – self-reflection is no longer conceived of as an innate ability but as a product of social life.

Secondly, equipped with the concept of role-taking and other associated notions (notably gesture, object, significant symbol, meaning and consciousness), Mead has left us a singularly inspiring conception of the self. The human being is a complex biological organism, whose rationality is intimately related to linguistic communication and social experience. Language is one of the central elements responsible for the emergence of the mind; it is not surprising, therefore, that Mead sees thinking as a sort of 'inner conversation'. For him, the self is not to be confused with the body. Rather, the self is a bio-social emergent whose evolution can be reconstructed from two different yet related points of view. From the perspective of the history of the species, Mead proposes an explanation of how self-consciousness gradually emerged as a composite product of both physiological developments and social intercourse. From the viewpoint of individual development, Mead's proposal revolves around the stages of 'play' and 'game'. Mead's self is thus a thoroughly social process, with two distinguishable phases, the 'I' (the self as our uncertain response to the situation) and the 'me' (the conscious self-image we construct by role-taking – that is, by adopting the attitude of the other).

Thirdly, the intersubjectivism that allows Mead to supersede Cartesian atomism without falling into the excesses of sociologism is founded upon a conception of the act that is irreducibly dialogical. Moreover, Mead's theory of the act locates the individual within the surrounding environment – *pace* Descartes, the self is not opposed to the world; rather, it is a part of it. Objects exert control over the act insofar as the perception at distance of an object (physical or social) not only constitutes a stimulus for action, but also controls the way we approach it: we incorporate the qualities of the perceived object in order to manipulate it in a successful fashion. In this sense, the character of the object determines to a large extent the way the act is organized. In a social act – that is, in a social interaction between multiple social objects – there is an adjustment between any person and the social object towards which that person acts, and such adjustment can be called social control. As the object controls the act, so social object controls the social act. Human conduct is socially influenced, much in the same manner as we are influenced when we approach the physical world we inhabit. By taking the attitude of an object I internalize its attitude towards me; in the case of society, by taking the attitude of the 'generalized other', I immediately become able to exert a certain amount of (social) control over my acts. Social control is thus but a form of self-criticism – social conventions control our actions as a result of our ability to take the attitude of the 'generalized other' through the 'me'.

The elegance and coherence of Mead's thinking is admirable. Despite the deplorable editorial state of Mead's writings, his system of philosophy deserves more credit than a mere early twentieth-century account of the origins of the self – it is an enduring exemplar of the promises of intersubjectivism. To read George Herbert Mead is an opportunity for current generations to engage in dialogue with an author who helped to found the discipline of sociology in spite of not having been a sociologist himself. The following chapters will attempt to provide a concise narrative of Mead's reception by later generations of social scientists, from sociologists to philosophers, in the US and abroad. As in any narrative, there will be protagonists, settings and a plot. So in the next chapter I shall discuss the influence of Mead's ideas in the context of American twentieth-century sociology. The protagonists in this episode will be the members of the Chicago school of sociology (Small, Thomas, Park, Cooley and Faris), as well as the sociologists whose work is associated with symbolic interactionism (Blumer, Strauss, Becker, Goffman). I will suggest that the interpretation which symbolic interactionists tend to give Mead, especially in the case of Blumer, is a form of legitimation of their own agenda rather than a balanced account of Mead's contributions. In the subsequent chapters I shall discuss a number of contemporary interpretations, so as to pave the way for a reassessment of Mead's contributions to social sciences today.

So let us turn now to the history of the reception of Mead's ideas in the work of his fellow sociologists at Chicago, before and after his demise in 1931.

6

Mead and Symbolic Interactionism

In this chapter I wish to make a diversion in the course of my discussion of Mead's ideas. So far I have been presenting my interpretation of his chief contributions to current social sciences. Now I suggest that we turn our attention to other authors' interpretations of Mead. Some of these readings, such as those of Herbert Blumer or Jürgen Habermas, have been so influential that they can be credited for having placed Mead in the sociological canon, side by side with Marx, Weber, Durkheim, Simmel and so on. But there is one particular claim I wish to make concerning the nature of 'canonization' processes. In my view, it is of the utmost importance that social practitioners and, in particular, undergraduate students increase their awareness regarding the historical and institutional nature of the processes through which some academic figures attained the status of 'classics'. Far from being an exception, Mead is a good example of this process. As I have argued elsewhere, the reception of his ideas in sociology provides us with an enlightening example of how the history of the discipline is influenced, not only by new ideas and systems, but also by the theoretical interests of their key interpreters.[1]

With this remark in mind, I now wish to suggest an account of the reception of Mead's ideas in twentieth-century American sociology. My argument focuses on two episodes. In the first place, I am going to situate Mead with reference to the so-called 'Chicago school' of sociology; secondly, I shall discuss the emergence of symbolic interactionism and the associated demise of the first Chicago school in the early 1950s. A critical analysis of Blumer's work will give me the opportunity to address one of the founding legends of American sociology, namely the Mead–Blumer relationship. Mead's role as a 'sociological classic', nowadays an established fact, should be seen as a historical process whose main agent was the American sociological current of 'symbolic interactionism', particularly through Mead's former student and research assistant, Herbert Blumer. It was Blumer who, more than anyone else, established Mead's reputation, in the 1950s and 1960s, as the single most innovative alternative to Talcott Parsons' structural functionalism – the then dominant sociological perspective. Along with Robert Merton's conception of 'middle-range' theories, Parsons' structural–functionalist perspective had established itself as the sociological paradigm, being at once the legitimate heir of the European founding fathers of sociology (Pareto, Durkheim and Weber) and the only truly scientific approach to sociological research. The early twentieth-century American sociological tradition, developed at the University of Chicago under the influence of philosophical pragmatism, was completely ignored in Parsons' seminal narrative of the origins and development of the discipline, the two-volume *The Structure of Social Action* (1938).[2] It is to this tradition that I now turn.

Mead and the Chicago school of sociology

A few words on the relation between philosophical pragmatism and the sociological tradition of symbolic interactionism will suffice to clarify why Mead's work, though not directly related to sociological themes or methods, has been revisited time and time again by sociologists in their search for a theoretical perspective which might represent a viable alternative to functionalism and structuralism. As Dmitri Shalin shows in his 'Pragmatism and Social Interactionism' (1986), there is an interface between pragmatism and interactionist sociology at a number of points:

1   it was from the pragmatist philosophical perspective on reality as being in the state of flux that social interactionism drew the inspiration to pursue the sociological study of the social order as an emergent process, as something always 'in-the-making';
2   the fundamental sociological notion of 'interaction' derives directly from the pragmatist philosophical attempt to supersede the traditional problem of the relation between the 'one' and the 'many' – the universal and the particulars – falling under it – through the conception of an 'emergent order';
3   the progressive and democratic values shared by most American pragmatists, Mead included, play a major role in the definition of the ideological underpinnings of interactionist sociology.[3]

In my view, these conceptual and thematic connections between pragmatism and interactionist sociology throw valuable light upon the relation between Mead and Chicago sociology.[4] By 'Chicago' I mean both the university, founded in 1892, and the city near Lake Michigan. As we have seen, Mead taught in the Department of Philosophy at the University of Chicago for over three decades. To a large extent, his influence over Chicago sociology is due to the enrolment of sociology students on his popular social psychology course. There is, however, a more important explanation for Mead's status as a central figure of the Chicago school, and this is his intellectual contribution to the problem of social interaction and self-consciousness, which he addressed from a pragmatist perspective.[5] If there is one common intellectual denominator among the various members of the Chicago school, bringing them together, this is philosophical pragmatism. In other words, Chicago sociologists during Mead's lifetime turned to pragmatism as a philosophical alternative to the utilitarianism which dominated most social sciences, especially economics: instead of the model of a single actor rationally pursuing his ends, pragmatism proposed the notion of a process relating the individual actor to the surrounding environment. This alliance between philosophical pragmatism and Chicago sociology remains one of the distinctive features of this sociological tradition, despite all the other influences it incorporated in the course of the second half of the twentieth century.

As to the city itself, it is fair to say that it provided the members of the sociology department with their main research material. The interest in social reform shared by most members of the Chicago school, including Mead, found a concrete setting in the community around the university. When Mead and his colleagues analysed social problems such as immigration, racism, urban planning, unemployment or education, their object of study was Chicago itself. At this time, Chicago was undergoing a rapid and profound process of urban growth, industrialization and social differentiation. Between the 1880s and the 1930s, the city became the final destination for hundreds of thousands of immigrants from Europe and other parts of the world. The 'progressive era', as this epoch became known later on, was indeed a period of great social transformation and Chicago was at the very heart of this societal process of change.[6]

Closely attuned to the growing metropolis, the vibrant new University of Chicago was the perfect institutional setting for a generation of social scientists concerned to offer scientific solutions to social problems. The Chicago school was very much oriented towards empirical studies of a quasi-ethnographic nature and towards social reform. Familiar with the sociological findings of Tönnies, Durkheim and Simmel, its members tried to establish the discipline by complementing European sociological theorizing and research methods with new insights; these were insights into the problems associated with the rapid modernization of the city of Chicago, and they were provided by American philosophical pragmatism. The contribution of the university's Department of Sociology and Anthropology (as it was officially designated at the time of its establishment in 1893) to the institutionalization of American sociology can hardly be underestimated. It includes the creation of the first academic journal in the field – the *American Journal of Sociology*, established in 1895; the foundation of the first American association of professional sociologists – the *American Sociological Society*, founded in 1905 and renamed *American Sociological Association* in 1959); the publication of textbooks such as Park and Burgess' *Introduction to the Science of Sociology* (1921), which helped to bring out a whole generation of professional sociologists; and the realization of numerous research projects. A case in point is the in-depth study by William I. Thomas and Florian Znaniecki of the Polish immigrant community, which led to the publication, in 1918, of the seminal study *The Polish Peasant in Europe and America*, probably the single best-known work of the first generation of the Chicago school.

What was Mead's influence upon his colleagues in the sociology department?[7] To put it in a different way, which aspect of the Chicago school approach to sociology shows best the influence of his social theory of the self? Mead's chief contribution to the school was nothing less than a wholly original conception of action and rationality. Rather than pointing to an alternative – in terms of its opposite – to the individualist conception of action typical of utilitarian social theory, and thus accepting the underlying dichotomy of action versus structure, of actor versus society, Mead questioned the very premises of the debate. In his view, there is no necessary opposition between the individual self and society. Human action can thus be conceived of as socially influenced *and* socially generative: individuals create the world around them just as they are moulded by it, in a continuous process of mutual construction. Social structures are, from Mead's innovative perspective, ongoing processes which simultaneously structure individual action and are structured by it. In other words, Mead's pragmatist model of action allows Chicago sociologists to reject both the individualism associated with utilitarian perspectives (still predominant in economics to this day) and the structuralism suggested by functionalism, systems theory and other sociological currents. I deeply agree with Joas when he observes that the true meaning of Mead's achievement lies 'in the fact that he fundamentally changed the way of looking at the problem' of the relationship between human agency and social structure.[8]

The demise of the first generation of the Chicago school is not to be explained solely in terms of the competition coming from Harvard (where Parsons would develop his career) and other Ivy League universities. Between the 1920s and the early 1930s, there was a debate among early interactionists that led to the dismemberment of the first Chicago school. According to the main historian of the school, Robert E. Faris, this debate opposed those who, like Mead, favoured a pragmatist articulation of body and mind against those who, like Cooley, were not so much preoccupied with avoiding the pitfalls of idealism as with promoting or undertaking sociological empirical research.[9] From this perspective, the cost of symbolic interactionism's success as a sociological tradition responsible for an enormous wealth of empirical research is the reification of the mind at the expense of the body. In order to understand Mead's role in this debate, one has to take into consideration the fact that his relationship with the Department of Sociology in the 1920s was personally mediated by two sociologists. It is their story that I now wish to discuss.

The first of those sociologists was Ellsworth Faris (1874–1953), the father of Robert Faris and himself a former student of Mead. Faris became the chairman of the sociology department after Small's retirement in 1926. Since joining the department in 1918 and particularly after becoming its head eight years later, Faris played a prominent role in establishing Mead's reputation among the post-1920 Chicago sociologists.[10] A teacher of considerable influence, he often advised sociology graduate students to attend Mead's lectures. As one of the graduate students recalled, Faris

> was very influential in taking his own students – who were students specializing in the area of social psychology inside the Department of Sociology – and directing them toward Mead's course. So, I would say that by all odds, this was the primary link between Mead in philosophy and the people in sociology at that time.[11]

The fact that this student's name was Herbert Blumer is not a trivial one. As Blumer recalled in a personal interview, it was through Faris that Mead became familiar with his dissertation, attended his doctoral examination (which took place in 1928 under Faris' chairmanship) and even questioned him.[12] Blumer subsequently joined the sociology faculty and in 1931 was asked by Mead to replace him in teaching his course on social psychology. Mead would die a few months later.

The relevance of this last episode stems from the fact that, until the very end of his life, Blumer would always claim to be Mead's intellectual heir because, at least in part, he had been Mead's last research assistant. This short yet personal relationship between Mead and Blumer has gained the status of a founding myth in the context of the self-legitimizing narrative of the origins and development of American sociology. As with any other myth, the narrative of the Blumer–Mead relationship performs two functions. On the one hand, it functions as an example of how a master–disciple relationship can contribute to the development of the discipline; on the other hand, it hides the discrepancies and contradictions that would disrupt the self-understanding of that discipline. In short, one has to go beyond the myth to understand fully the actual nature and implications of the connection between Mead's social pragmatism and Blumer's symbolic interactionism. This is what I propose to do next.

Blumer's Mead: a classic in the making

Herbert Blumer (1900–1987) began his pilgrimage to pragmatism well before he met Mead in Chicago.[13] Charles Ellwood, a devoted follower of Dewey, was the first intellectual reference for the young Blumer. It was under Ellwood that Blumer took his BA and MA in sociology, in 1920 and 1921 respectively, at the University of Missouri. Blumer then began his career as a sociology instructor in Missouri, where he worked under Ellwood until 1924; then he moved to Chicago, to study for his PhD. Blumer arrived at Chicago already acquainted with the pragmatists' social reformist agenda and anti-Cartesian philosophical stance. The fact that he hesitated to name Ellwood as his first intellectual mentor is certainly associated with the latter's 'abstract, value-oriented perspective'.[14] While at Chicago, Blumer was exposed to a much more empirically inclined sociology through the teaching of Faris, whose role in the relationship between Mead and the young Blumer has already been noted. As Blumer recalls: 'I was introduced to Mead's thought through my studies with Ellsworth Faris. Later I worked directly with Mead over a period of several years, serving part of this time as his research assistant.'[15] In Mead's work, Blumer discovered a perspective of the human condition that would accompany him throughout his career, and which he develops at the University of California-Berkeley from 1952 until his death in 1987. In order to determine the extent to which Blumer modified his master's theses in order to cope better with the intellectual and research challenges of the 1950s and 1960s, I will examine in the following paragraphs the main features of Blumer's sociological perspective in contrast to Mead's own proposals.

Blumer's life-long intellectual interest is the relation between theory and empirical research in the social sciences. This theme can be found as early as in his doctoral dissertation ('The Method of Social Psychology', 1928), and recurs in virtually all his major writings. At first, Blumer endorsed a methodological position which is closer to the experimental scientific method espoused by Mead. As he asserts in his PhD dissertation, 'there is nothing in human behavior which prevents the application of the natural scientific method to human behavior'.[16] In the course of the 1930s, Blumer gradually moves towards a position which can be seen as a reconstruction of Cooley's 'sympathetic introspection'. Despite rejecting Cooley's mentalism, Blumer wholeheartedly adheres to his inclination towards participant observation. In other words, Blumer comes to endorse the thesis, associated with the work of Cooley, Thomas and others, that the interpretation of the social actor's actions and of the meaning that actor attributes to them is of paramount importance to the social scientist. To understand social reality one has to immerse oneself into the web of social relations and try to see the world as the social actor does. Blumer's reputation rose dramatically during the 1930s, due to a distinctive way of reconciling this predilection for interpretative methodologies with a theoretical approach sensitive to the symbolic nature of the social world. At a time when sociology was establishing itself as an academic discipline by means of extensive quantitative data analysis and survey research (tendencies which World War II would only intensify), Blumer's *verstehen* research strategy filled a disciplinary niche. His perspective has to be understood, from its very inception, as an alternative to Talcott Parsons' structural functionalism, the dominant perspective in American sociology until the end of the 1960s. As a consequence, Mead's inclusion in the sociological canon would be conditioned, for better or for worse, by this circumstance.

Assuming a critical position vis-à-vis Thomas and Znaniecki's methodological perspective,[17] Blumer puts forth an alternative which focuses exclusively on the action-problems located in what Park called the 'moral order'. In 1937,[18] Blumer coins the expression 'symbolic interactionism'. This expression came to describe a current of sociological research which was concerned not so much with the relationship of the physical environment to social experience as with the subjective aspects of social life – that is, with the symbolic texture of collective action. In particular, symbolic interaction should be seen as a 'generative and formative agency in its own right'.[19] This insight, reminiscent of Mead's ideas on symbolization, gained an enormous currency among sociologists in the 1960s, inspiring such notable works as Berger and Luckmann's *Social Construction of Reality*. This circumstance makes the following questions all the more pertinent: what does it mean, exactly, to say that symbolic interaction is a formative agency, and what are its implications for empirical sociological research?

To begin with, symbolic interactionism is founded upon three basic premises. The first is that individuals act towards the things that compose their world (physical objects, human beings, or institutions) on the basis of the meanings these things have for them. The second premise states that the meaning of these things is a social emergent, that is, it arises from social interaction. The third refers to the fact that these meanings are continuously under modification in the course of the interpretative process by means of which actors deal with the surrounding environment.[20] Elaborating on the implications of these premises, Blumer identifies the six 'root images' or basic elements which distinguish symbolic interactionism from other analytical perspectives. The first basic element is the conception of human society as composed of 'people engaging in action'.[21] The pragmatist underpinnings of symbolic interactionism are clear. The second root image refers to the nature of social interaction. At this point Blumer makes a claim of central importance. He rejects the study of social action as the product of the influence of one or more external factors. Rather, following Mead's insights on this matter, individual action is to be construed as resulting from the interaction between actors. By recovering Mead's theory, Blumer wishes to found his model of action upon a conceptual structure more amenable to interpretative methodologies than the dominant 'factorial approaches', of which Parsons' paradigm is an example. The third root image is related to the nature of objects. An object, according to Blumer, is 'anything that can be indicated or referred to'. Thus Blumer's conception is similar to Mead's insofar as both see human experience as the result of a process in which individuals create, transform and cast aside the objects that form their world.[22]

There are three further root images, all related to the model of action in symbolic interactionism: the 'human being as an acting organism', the 'nature of human action' and the 'interlinkage of action'. As in the case of the image of human beings as acting organisms, one should emphasize that symbolic interactionists tend to conceive of human beings not as entities determined by sociological or social-psychological factors, but as organisms which interact with each other through a social process of making indications to themselves. In other words, Blumer recovers Mead's insight that what defines a human being is the ability to see oneself as an object. This very notion is the basis of the fifth root image in symbolic interactionism. It is the human ability to envision oneself as an object that explains why interpretation is so important for Blumer's conception of human action: being able to see itself as an object, the self forges a line of conduct on the basis of how it interprets the world. The sixth and final root image is a generalization of this insight. As individual actors direct their lines of action according to their interpretation of the things they encounter in the course of their activities, so, too, large-scale social phenomena are the product of the interlinkage or interconnectedness of individual lines of conduct. An example might clarify Blumer's point. Even in the case of a large-scale phenomenon as industrialization, he contends that this societal process can be understood as the outcome of a great number of interlinked or 'joint' acts.[23] From this perspective, industrialization is to be seen as a macro-sociological process, which emerges from the articulation of multiple micro-sociological acts. Individual actors such as a manual labourer or the CEO of a large corporation contribute, through their 'careers' as social actors, to the definition and development of large-scale phenomena of which they are only partially aware. In sum, Blumer suggests that intertwined patterns of action and interaction lie at the origin of large-scale social phenomena. In this he argues against the factorial approaches, which neglect the formative character of symbolization.

In order to promote an alternative to the dominant factorial approaches, Blumer proposes to make explicit the theoretical scheme of human society implicit in Mead's writings. In my view, his attempt at rendering Mead's ideas relevant as an alternative to these factorial approaches entails a certain measure of creative reading which is not without its problems. This is not to say that Blumer did not get Mead right. My contention is not related to the accuracy of Blumer's interpretation; rather, my point is that Mead's legacy for contemporary social theory is not limited to the contributions emphasized by Blumer. In particular, Mead's contributions should not be reduced to an argument over the ownership of a sociological perspective which reverses Parsons' emphasis on social order and prioritizes, instead, *agency* over *structure*. On the contrary, Mead's seminal contribution is to suggest a completely different way of looking at the problem.

Assuming the role of Mead's intellectual heir, Blumer reconstructs the sociological implications of his thought by discussing a number of central matters. These central matters include the self, the act, social interaction, objects and joint action. According to Blumer, Mead's picture of the human being as an actor revolves around the ability to interact with oneself by means of 'making indications to himself and meeting these indications by making further indications'.[24] As such, in Blumer's view, Mead's social actor

> ceases to be a responding organism whose behavior is a product of what plays upon him from the outside, the inside, or both. Instead, he acts toward his world, interpreting what confronts him and organizing his action on the basis of the interpretation.[25]

Not surprisingly, Blumer suggests that there stems a way of viewing 'human action' from this conception of the self – a way which is centred on the process of self-interaction. That is, action is built up in the process of coping with the world: '[b]y making indications to himself and by interpreting what he indicates, the human being has to forge or piece together a line of action'.[26] In other words, for Blumer and his followers, human action is a social phenomenon whose rationale is closely related to the individual's ability to interpret the world. As such, Blumer maintains, sociological analysis should focus on the 'defining process' by means of which the social actors construct their lines of action. It is difficult not to see the similitude between Blumer's position and the methodological proposals advanced by Thomas ('definition of the situation') and Cooley ('sympathetic introspection').

This similitude is even more apparent in the case of 'social interaction' – another one of the topics crucial to Mead from which Blumer proposes to retrieve a relevant contribution to his own theories. Referring back to Mead's distinction between a 'non-conscious conversation of gestures' and a 'conscious conversation of gestures' (now labelled 'symbolic interaction'), Blumer argues that Mead understood symbolic interaction as involving '*interpretation*, or ascertaining the meaning of the actions or remarks of the other person, and *definition*, or conveying indications to another person as to how he is to act'.[27] In other words, Blumer's Mead is said to conceive of symbolic interaction as a formative process through which meaning is created. Blumer's interpretation, however, runs counter to Mead's own words in this respect. As we have seen, Mead argues that the meaning of the significant symbol is 'present in the social act before the emergence of consciousness or awareness of meaning occurs'.[28] This contradicts Blumer's contention that meaning is created *as a consequence of* the social actor's interpretative act. Blumer is of the view that interpretation is a process of self-indication in which the social actor 'makes an object of what it notes, gives it a meaning, and uses the meaning as the basis for directing its action',[29] whereas Mead ascertains that meaning 'is not to be conceived, fundamentally, as a state of consciousness . . . on the contrary, it should be conceived objectively, as having its existence entirely within this field [of experience]'.[30]

Blumer's reason for opting for a creative interpretation of Mead is in his own theoretical agenda. Writing at a time when Parsons' structural functionalism was the predominant sociological perspective, Blumer saw in Mead the source of inspiration necessary to build up an alternative to Parsons' model. As I have suggested above, at the core of the alternative he proposed lies the idea that symbolic interaction constitutes a formative process in its own right. It is now time to discuss the implications of this claim. Despite the distance between Mead's conception of meaning and Blumer's nominalist version, the latter was able to draw from Mead's work the insights he needed to construct a robust alternative to Parsons' proposals.

Blumer's notion of symbolic interaction, understood as a social process in which participants build up their respective lines of conduct by constant interpretation of each other's actions, has proved to be a fruitful research tool. It has been the inspiring motif for an entire generation of social scientists interested in going beyond the objectivist limits imposed by the cumulative and quantitative model in sociology. Covering similar ground to Schutz's phenomenology of the social world, Blumer put forth a picture of society as consisting of what is forged by the social actor out of the things she perceives, interprets and judges. Instead of a social order maintained by a set of cultural norms imposed upon individual members, Blumer proposes a society in which social actors construct the world around them by means of the dual process of interpretation and definition. Furthermore, Blumer asserts that symbolic interaction defined in this way is able to cover the full range of human relationships, from the simplest form of face-to-face interaction to the most complex institutional process.

In my opinion, the chief merit of symbolic interactionism lies in its methodological perspective and in the enormous wealth of empirical research it has been able to inspire up to this day. Of course, Mead's own methodological preferences, closer as they are to the experimental method of the natural sciences, have little or nothing to do with Blumer's sympathetic–introspective method. Still, from the point of view of the fruitfulness of Mead's ideas, it is noteworthy that Blumer is able to make use of his notion of 'taking the role of the other' in order to develop an interpretative methodological strategy. Blumer's contention is clear. Since social actors act toward their world on the basis of how they see it and not on the basis of how that world appears to the outside observer, the sociologist has no choice but to 'take the role of the actor and see his world from his standpoint'.[31]

An interpretative methodological framework is much more suited to the investigation of small, close human associations than to the study of macro-social processes such as large corporations, bureaucracy, warfare and international relations. The same limitations apply to social, cultural or economic structures, which evolve gradually in the course of centuries and can become as large as the entire planet (as in the case of Immanuel Wallerstein's world-system). Blumer tries to meet these criticisms by pointing out that both large social acts and large social structures, however complex they may be, require symbolic interaction throughout their entire histories.[32] I believe Blumer goes some way towards meeting the criticisms in question, but there are those who argue that he does not go far enough. Some of the critics of symbolic interactionism point out that there is in it a systematic neglect of themes such as power, structures (economic, political, etc.) and other material components of society. Given the fact that Blumer blurs the distinction between Mead's thinking and his own proposals, this sort of criticism is also frequently directed towards Mead himself.

Thus Mead's inclusion in the sociological canon is something that Blumer and his followers can take credit for, but it has been achieved at a high cost. Mead has been portrayed as the main social thinker responsible for a view of human society in terms of symbolic interaction. As a consequence of the partial character of Blumer's interpretation, Mead's writings on subjects such as the experimental method, temporality, democratic theory and communicative ethics, not to mention his personal involvement in numerous civic activities throughout his life, have been examined only in specialized literature and even today remain almost absent from sociology textbooks. Blumer's Mead can be rightly accused of 'idealism', that is, of systematically neglecting the material dimensions of the reproduction of society. This accusation is not, however, substantiated if one takes Mead's own writings into account.[33] Moreover, Blumer's Mead conceals Mead's greatest contribution to twentieth-century social theory, namely his wholly innovative and original way of looking at the problem of reconciling agency and structure. Instead of construing these categories as poles in a rigid and insurmountable dichotomy, Mead has taught us to see them as different elements of the same, dynamic, 'always in-the-making' process. In other words, Mead's rejection of the traditional dichotomy between realism and nominalism is closely associated with his distinctively pragmatist approach to the old philosophical problem of universals and particulars. In response to the question: 'Should one study the "one" (society, structure, the universal) or focus instead in the "many" (individuals, agency, particulars)?', Mead always insisted that neither should be given primacy; instead, one should conceive of individuals and of society as being engaged in a mutually constitutive relation.

Meadian sociology: some examples

In what follows, I am going to present and discuss four examples of sociological approaches which explicitly positioned themselves in a direct line of intellectual descent from Mead's social-psychological ideas: the 'Iowa School' associated with the work of Manford Kuhn, Anselm Strauss' 'negotiated order approach', the 'labelling theory' developed by Howard S. Becker, and Erving Goffman's 'dramaturgical approach'. Of course, several other sociological perspectives that draw on Mead's ideas could have been chosen. The reason why I selected these four particular strands is related to their influence and relevance. Especially in the 1960s and 1970s, these neo-Meadian sociologies were, along with Blumer's own perspective, the main currents inside the symbolic interactionist paradigm. Together they offer a good picture of how diverse a sociology developed under the influence of Mead can be – which is perhaps the best testimony to the richness of his ideas.

In stark opposition to Blumer's naturalistic interpretative approach, an alternative strand of Meadian sociology emerged around the work of Manford Kuhn: the so-called 'Iowa school' (which owes much to Kuhn's stay at Iowa between 1946 until his death in 1963). One finds at the centre of this school's agenda the attempt to draw on Mead's work in order to develop a quantitative, experimental variant of symbolic interactionism. Kuhn and his Iowa followers distinguish themselves from their interactionist counterparts at Chicago through their emphasis on making Meadian concepts such as the self, or the social object, operational in such a way as to permit the definition of empirically tested hypotheses. The best-known example of this attempt is the 'twenty statements test' (TST), in which respondents are asked to fill out twenty blank spaces completing the sentence 'I am:'.[34] The TST is supposed to capture the individual's sense of self in a deterministic and generalizable way. It is not difficult to acknowledge the enormous gulf that separates Blumer's Chicago school, with its emphasis on participant observation research techniques, from Kuhn's Iowa school, oriented as it is to the quantitative analysis of hypotheses concerning functional relations between self and groups.

One finds a clear expression of Kuhn's realist orientation in his 1964 paper 'Major Trends in Symbolic Interaction Theory in the Past Twenty-Five Years'.[35] Kuhn begins by identifying a purported 'contradiction between *determinacy* and *indeterminacy* in Mead's over-all point of view',[36] which is supposed to stem from Mead's account of the social and linguistic nature of the self (the deterministic aspect of his theory, according to Kuhn) and the 'I–me distinction' (for Kuhn, the unpredictable nature of the 'I' concurred to the indeterminate aspect of Mead's views). This supposed contradiction permits Kuhn to assess the state of the art in interactionist sociology in the early 1960s. Some theories and authors are labelled 'indeterminate' on account of exploring those aspects of Mead's work which are less amenable to quantitative analysis – for instance Erving Goffman's dramaturgical approach and Becker's sociology of deviance are given as examples of interactionist theories presupposing indeterminacy); others are presented as doing the exact opposite. Not surprisingly, perhaps, Kuhn concludes his paper by predicting for the 'next twenty-five years of symbolic interaction theory an accelerated development of research techniques on the one hand, and a coalescing of most of the separate subtheories under consideration in this paper on the other'.[37]

This exercise in historical prediction did not prove too successful. What actually happened was pretty much the opposite of Kuhn's expectations. Despite the important work of Carl J. Couch, who developed a research programme on the generic principles of collective action, adopting a 'laboratorial ethnography' methodology,[38] the fact is that the symbolic interactionist tradition evolved in a direction which is closer to Blumer's naturalistic and qualitative perspective. Of course, one can wonder whether 'tradition' is the most adequate concept to describe all the work being done under the label of 'symbolic interactionism', given the enormous variety of methodological and theoretical orientations among the interactionists.

One of these naturalistic–qualitative proposals can be found in the work of Anselm Strauss (1916–96), a former student of Blumer and Howard Hughes at Chicago. Strauss owes much of his reputation to the 'negotiated order approach', arguably one of the most productive developments in social interactionist sociology in the last few decades. A brief discussion of this approach suffices to show how Mead's ideas were mobilized to build original and productive sociological perspectives. In *Negotiations* (1978), Strauss seeks to offer a paradigm that other researchers can qualify, amend and work on, so that eventually a theory of the 'negotiated order' may develop. Departing from the sympathetic–introspective method suggested by Blumer, Strauss believes that 'it is not sufficient to pay attention to an actor's perceptions of the potential efficacy of chosen modes (including negotiation); they require analysis in terms of those more embracing conceptions of society'.[39] With this proviso in mind, he then analyses the research of a number of social scientists, including Erving Goffman (whose work will be discussed later in this chapter), from the perspective of their treatment of the category of 'negotiation'. Strauss concludes that social scientists in general tend to overlook the fact that social orders are to be conceived of as negotiated orders. In order to avoid this difficulty, he proposes a paradigm of negotiation comprising the following insights. Firstly, social orders are always, in some sense, negotiated orders. The qualification 'in some sense' denotes Strauss' contention that negotiations are general social phenomena always found in conjunction with other social processes – namely coercion, persuasion or manipulation. Secondly, specific negotiation processes always take place within larger social settings. As he puts it, 'larger structural considerations need to be explicitly linked with microscopic analysis of negotiation processes'.[40] Thirdly, since negotiations are thought to be relatively universal phenomena, Strauss' paradigm has to be able to deal with the whole range of types of negotiations. This implies the examination of a variety of structural contexts and their associated courses of negotiation.

In a clear demonstration that Mead and the Chicago tradition of sociology can inspire work which is not limited to Blumer's model, Strauss' paradigm is deeply committed to the articulation between the analysis of specific negotiation processes and larger structural considerations. In particular, Strauss suggests that the study of negotiation processes should pay attention to 'subprocesses of negotiation' (such as making trade-offs, obtaining kickbacks, paying off debts and the like) and to the 'structural context', within which negotiations take place. Regarding this latter element, Strauss does not hesitate to contradict his former Chicago professor by claiming that 'the structural properties [are] entering very directly *as conditions* into the course of the negotiation itself':[41] in other words, he swiftly puts aside Blumer's criticisms of the 'factorial approaches' for the sake of answering other critics, who accused symbolic interactionism of being insensitive to structural conditions. Moreover, it can be argued that this is exactly why Strauss' negotiated order is as much an intellectual descendant from Mead's writings as Blumer's ideas. Indeed, David Maines rightly observes that Mead's theory of temporality, by emphasizing the structuring effect that the past has upon the present, presents us with a dialectical view encompassing both structure and process, determinacy and indeterminacy. It is that dialectical perspective that lies at the base of the negotiated order, and that appears in a number of studies informed by that perspective.[42]

In other words, Strauss' negotiated-order paradigm explicitly tries to overcome the realist–nominalist dichotomy, an attempt that, in my view, is closer to Mead's position than Blumer's proposals.

The same cannot be said, however, of our next exemplar of Meadian sociology: Howard S. Becker, whose main contribution to interactionist theory is the work on deviance he has been developing ever since the publication of his hugely influential *Outsiders* in 1963.

Becker's labelling perspective has been a major source of inspiration for many criminologists working within the interactionist paradigm in the last few decades. My aim in what follows is to discuss his proposals as a symbolic interactionist contribution to the sociology of deviance. Mead and Blumer are the only two authors to whom Becker does make explicit reference when he writes on the intellectual influences behind his conception of deviance as collective action.[43] How should this action be investigated? Becker contends, in a manner which is reminiscent of Mead's ideas on the principles of the experimental method, that all the individual perspectives involved in any episode of alleged deviance should be taken into account by the social scientist. From this point of view, deviance is not to be seen 'as an isolated act whose origin we are to discover'; rather, Becker emphasizes, 'the act alleged to occur, when it has occurred, takes place in a complex network of acts involving others, and takes on some of that complexity because of the way various people and groups define it'.[44]

One can already guess at the processual character of Becker's conception of deviance from this last remark. In other words, Becker argues that sociology should study deviant collective acts by means of a model that allows for change through time. This sequential model of deviance results from cross-classifying kinds of behaviour and the responses they evoke. In particular, Becker defines four theoretical types of deviance. Two of them are relatively straightforward. When a behaviour is not perceived as deviant and indeed obeys the rule, it is 'conforming behaviour'; when one acts in such a way as to disobey the rule and at the same time be perceived as doing so, one is engaging in a 'pure deviant behaviour'. But the other two types deserve a closer look. The 'falsely accused' type characterizes a situation in which a person, despite not having committed any improper action, is perceived by others as having done so. Much to the contrary, 'secret deviance', the fourth and final type, occurs when 'an improper act is committed, yet no one notices it or reacts to it as a violation of the rules'.[45] This last theoretical type is not only the most interesting kind of deviance but is also the most problematic, at least in the light of the theoretical perspective behind Becker's sequential model of deviance.

This perspective is 'labelling theory', the interactionist alternative to the functionalist analysis of the phenomenon of deviance. Functionalism discriminates between those types of behaviour which are functional (i.e. promote stability) and those which are not (i.e. disrupt stability). Unlike it, labelling theory conceives of deviance as the failure to obey group orders. Becker contends, in particular, that *social groups create deviance by making the rules whose infraction constitutes deviance*, and by applying those rules to particular people and labelling them as outsiders'.[46] In other words, Becker wishes to convey the idea that deviance is not a quality of the act the person commits, but rather a consequence of a labelling process: a 'deviant act' is an act that people label as such. Wholly in the spirit of symbolic interactionism, labelling theory defines deviance not as an intrinsic quality of a given behaviour, but as the product of the interaction between the person who commits an act and those who react to it.

At this point, though, a problem seems to arise. If, as Becker argues, only acts which are regarded as deviant by others are really deviant, 'secret deviance' (the fourth type mentioned above) seems to be self-contradictory; for how can an act be deviant if no-one has defined it as such? This paradox resolves itself as soon as we take into consideration the sequential character of Becker's model. Deviance, as all other forms of collective action, takes place over time. More specifically, definitions of what constitutes deviance occur sequentially: the very same act might be defined as non-deviant at $T1$ and deviant at $T2$. As Becker explains, a collective action such as sado-masochistic fetishism might not be 'secretly deviant' at $T1$ because the existing rules would not take it as deviant, but might be 'secretly deviant' at $T2$ 'because, a new rule having been made in the interim, a procedure now existed which would allow that determination'.[47] As the social construction of rules evolves over time, so does what is considered deviant and what is not. A sociological analysis that ignores the 'career' of deviant acts (which begins with subscribing to a nonconforming rule and ends with joining an organized deviant group, after several intermediary stages) is unable to tackle the 'power' dimension involved in these phenomena. For, if there is a founding insight behind any interactionist empirical study of deviance, that insight is that social rules are the creation of specific social groups. The structure of power relations in any given concrete society assumes a pivotal importance in the interactionist theory of deviance.

In short, Becker's model of deviance is symbolic interactionism's alternative to the dominant structural functionalism developed mainly at Harvard and Columbia in the 1950s and 1960s. As such, it has designed a highly successful research programme; for it has paved the way for an entire generation of criminologists and social psychologists. But Mead's influence on this model is limited. True, Blumer's Mead has exerted a certain amount of influence on Becker, but Becker's own line of research cannot be said to have much of a direct contact with Mead. Becker's central objective is to put forth an interactionist approach to deviance, which might be readily applied to empirical sociological studies. Labelling theory is a culturalist approach which, by emphasizing the importance of the imposition of definitions by certain privileged groups in society, offers indeed a stimulating and fresh look at the problem of deviance. The filiation of ideas here is quite intricate; rather than relating it simplistically to Mead, one should regard this approach as a fascinating development of Blumer's work on the sociological implications of Mead's ideas.

If the influence of Mead on Becker's work has been profoundly mediated and shaped by Blumer's interactionism, there is to be found, at the margins of the Chicago school, an author whose relation to Mead is even less apparent. Erving Goffman (1922–82), one of the most original theorists of everyday social life, hardly ever makes use of Mead. And yet Goffman's dramaturgical approach to social reality can be said to be a brilliant exploration of some of the themes initially investigated by Mead. I refer to such concepts as the self, social interaction, social order or social inequality. I am going to give now a brief account of Goffman's theory of face-to-face interaction, presented side by side with Mead's social theory of the self. As we shall see, one can draw illuminating parallels between Mead's social psychology and Goffman's dramaturgical approach. The latter is, I would say, a highly original re-elaboration of some of the insights explored by Mead decades before.

The self as product of dramatic performance is, arguably, Goffman's favoured metaphor in accounting for the nature of the self: for Goffman, the self is constantly defined through the performances staged in social life. These performances, in turn, are more or less constrained by the ritual order of society, which depends on the specific type of social establishment. As we follow the social rules and present ourselves according to our 'place' or status in the hierarchy, we help the ritual order of social life to be preserved. This interactional work is oriented to maintaining the dignity of social actors; Goffman calls it 'face-work'. In none of his other books is this dramaturgical model more profoundly explored than in *The Presentation of Self in Everyday Life* (1959). There Goffman offers his readers a sort of handbook, detailing a sociological perspective from which life in social establishments can be studied. The perspective in question is that of theatrical performance; the book's chief topic is the set of techniques employed by social actors to guide and control the impression which others form of them. Goffman outlines six dramaturgical principles: performances, teams, regions, discrepant roles, communication out of character and impression management. I would like to emphasize the importance of 'performance' in what defines Goffman's conception of the self. A performance refers to 'the activity of an individual which occurs during a period marked by his continuous presence before a particular set of observers and which has some influence on the observers'.[48] Goffman comes close to suggesting that all social life is a real-life drama. In particular, he argues that it is impossible to distinguish a person's self from that person's performance. For example, in order to be a college professor it is necessary not only to possess certain attributes (e.g. the required academic qualifications), but also to play the part successfully. It is the credibility of this performance that leads the audience and the social actor to impute a self to a performed character.

The dual self one finds in Goffman's work is somewhat indebted to Mead's ideas. Goffman apprehends Mead's distinction between the 'I' and the 'me' and transforms it, making it serve the needs of his dramaturgy. Thus, in *The Presentation of the Self*, Goffman introduces the 'crucial discrepancy between our all-too-human selves and our socialized selves'.[49] But, as I will try to show next, this 'discrepancy', though reminiscent of Mead's distinction between the 'I' and the 'me', should be seen as an entirely original proposal. To Goffman, the 'all-too-human self', also called 'self-as-performer', relates to the basic motivational core which leads us to engage in performances. This self-as-performer is more than a dramatic effect. Its attributes are psycho-biological (e.g. impulses, moods and other psychic energies). This explains why Goffman locates here the human being capable of fantasizing, dreaming, thinking, feeling pride or shame. On the other hand, there is the 'socialized self' or the 'self-as-character': this part of the self is a social product. To Goffman, the socialized self, not the self-as-performer, represents what we think of as our inner self. He explains this counter-intuitive thesis in the following manner:

> A correctly staged and performed character leads the audience to impute a self to a performed character, but this imputation – this self – is a product of a scene that comes off, and is not a *cause* of it. The self, then, as a performed character, is not an organic unit that has a specific location . . . it is a dramatic effect arising diffusely from a scene that is presented, and the characteristic issue, the crucial concern, is whether it will be credited or discredited.[50]

This passage is an eloquent example of how Goffman conceives of the self. It is also testimony of the distance that separates Goffman's dramaturgical theory of the self from Mead's social psychology. In my view, it is hardly a coincidence that the notion of 'role' constitutes a strategic vantage point from which to confront these two authors' models of the self. While it is the case that Mead often uses the expression 'to take the role of the other', the fact remains that he explicitly rules out its theatrical implications. 'This latter phrase', says Mead, speaking about role-taking, 'is a little unfortunate because it suggests an actor's attitude which is actually more sophisticated than that which is involved in our own experience'; and then he adds: 'To this degree it does not correctly describe that which I have in mind'.[51] The reason why Mead rejects using the theatrical metaphor to illustrate his conception of the self is simple. All he wishes to convey with the expression 'taking the role of the other' is that, when a person adopts the role of another person, she gains an added control over her own response – which contributes to a smoother social interaction. To put it in slightly different terms, one could say that, for Mead, the distance between the person (self-as-performer) and the mask (self-as-character) is minimal. For Goffman, on the contrary, it could hardly be larger.

In *Presentation of the Self*, a role is a fabricated performance. More importantly, at least for our present purposes, performances can be either cynical (if the performer does not believe in the character being played) or sincere (if she does). A crucial part of the performances is the 'front', which defines the situation for those watching it. Within the front, Goffman distinguishes between 'setting' (the physical scene: say, a classroom) and the 'personal front', which includes both 'expressive equipment' (speech, clothes and so on) and 'manner' (stimuli which warn the audience about the nature of the performance). In 'Role Distance' (1961), Goffman further explores the sociological implications of the concept of role.

Of the various types of roles Goffman identifies, 'role-distance' is certainly the most important. 'Role-distance', which refers to the individual's ability to remain separate from roles whose 'virtual self' displeases them, expresses better than any other concept the chief insight of Goffman's dramaturgy. The self is not the person behind the mask. There is no 'real' self behind the 'contrived', performed self. The masks individuals use in their performances are as much a part of their self as the motivational core responsible for staging a performance: the distinction between self-as-performer and self-as-character is thus superfluous. The fact that people are able to distance themselves from some of the roles in which they are involved is an indication of two different things. Firstly, Goffman's social actor can be (and often is) a cynical agent, free from the moral constrains associated with a sincere performance. Secondly, the self is a social process, a process whose dramaturgical nature Goffman never ceases to emphasize.

On the contrary, Mead's conception of the self does not comprise such a theatrical dimension. When Mead speaks about 'taking the role of the other', he is not referring to a complex pattern of behaviour such as the sociological notion of 'role' might suggest; rather, what he has in mind is a behavioural disposition to respond to a given stimulus the same way another would – that is, an attitude. Mead's notion of role-taking is limited to the anticipation of the other's behaviour, it does not extend to the adoption of her persona in a complex and organized social situation. Mead's conception of the self seems to confirm this point. His self is not a dramatic effect. It is a socially determined biological organism. As such, it does not emerge as a product of performances in social situations. In short, Mead's self is as much a bodily organism (as the impulsive 'I' shows), as it is an entity moulded by the society in which he lives (as the 'generalized other' and the 'me' attest).

Goffman's conception of self has been the inspiring motif of numerous fascinating sociological studies on the dramaturgical aspects of social interaction. Mead's model of the self, on the other hand, has expressed as no other the philosophical implications of the sociality of human action. And yet the link connecting these two authors' work is, at best, fragile. It all goes to show that Mead's influence over symbolic interactionism is far from providing a common intellectual denominator for a certain sociological current. Rather, the relationship between Mead and symbolic interactionism is much more subtle and complex than that perspective would imply. In my view, it should be seen either as a mediated relationship (via Blumer's reading), or as a starting point for original proposals, as Goffman's example suggests.

In any case, Mead's association with symbolic interactionism does show the fecundity of his thought. This is not so much a question of how accurately the authors in question have interpreted his words, as one of acknowledging the breadth of sociological research developed under his influence. The diversity of the lines of inquiry which have started under the label of 'symbolic interactionism' only reinforces the idea that this second generation of the Chicago school, now working away from that city and its university, followed Mead's insights in completely new and exciting ways. Goffman's dramaturgy is a most eloquent illustration of my thesis.

In this chapter we have discussed the role played by Mead's ideas in the genesis and development of symbolic interactionism. In particular, it has been suggested that the classical pragmatist answer to the problem of reconciling realism and nominalism, which Mead wholeheartedly endorsed, is as relevant today as it was when it was first formulated. Thus questions such as Gary Alan Fine's, concerning 'the chasm between an interpretivist and a social realist approach' within contemporary symbolic interactionism – 'Are they still wings of a single perspective in a meaningful sense when they cannot agree on epistemology: whether the world is ultimately knowable?'[52] – admit of one answer only, if we were to follow the pragmatists on this matter. Symbolic interactionists should begin by rejecting such a dichotomic discursive framework and turn instead towards theoretical and methodological perspectives which reject the analytical primacy of either individual or society: if there is a philosophical lesson to be drawn by contemporary symbolic interactionists from classic pragmatists, this is the rejection of rigid dichotomies. The individual, as Mead once wrote, 'constitutes society as genuinely as society constitutes the individual'.[53] This seemingly insignificant remark, to which every contemporary social scientist would in principle subscribe, is in fact one of the most vital of Mead's neglected insights.

7

Mead and Twentieth-Century Sociology

As we have seen in the previous chapter, Mead's influence on American sociology until the 1970s was predominantly mediated by symbolic interactionism. It is through the work of authors such as Blumer, Strauss and Becker that his model of the self has gained currency among sociologists, in the US and abroad. This is not to say, however, that symbolic interactionists are the only social theorists interested in exploring the implications of Mead's thinking for contemporary purposes. In this chapter I examine the deployment of Mead's ideas in the writings of several leading twentieth-century thinkers, such as Arnold Gehlen, Jürgen Habermas, Axel Honneth, Hans Joas, Randall Collins and Jeffrey Alexander. None of these authors is directly associated with the tradition of symbolic interactionism, yet they all have come across Mead's work at one point or another in their careers, providing in some cases crucially important re-examinations of his contributions. The aim of these fairly brief discussions is to clarify the ongoing influence of Mead's ideas on today's social theory.

Arnold Gehlen

Apart from Durkheim, who in 1913 and 1914 gave some critical lectures on the subject (though they were only published in 1955),[1] one of the very first European authors to show an interest in American philosophical pragmatism was the German philosopher Max Scheler (1874–1928). In Scheler's *Knowledge and Work* (1926), in spite of his acceptance of pragmatism's axiom that knowledge is bound up with action, one finds a note of criticism towards this philosophical tradition:

the spirit that permeated pragmatism [was] the same spirit that spoke from the eleven-story buildings of Chicago, from the verses of Walt Whitman – a spirit that must have remained left over from the unre-strained puritan work ethic, which created America in the first place and which, as Max Weber said, brought forth the 'age of heroes of early capi-talism' in Geneva and Holland, after his original, Christian-calvinist superstructure was destroyed.[2]

For all of Scheler's misleading description of pragmatism as a primitive form of utilitarianism, it was through his work that his countryman Arnold Gehlen (1904–76) became acquainted with this philosophical current – only in a much more productive way. Arnold Gehlen made extensive use of Mead's theory of the self in the 1950 edition of his major work, *Man: His Nature and Place in the World* (1940), thus intro-ducing Mead to German audiences. Gehlen's reading is, however, highly selective, as he retrieves from Mead's writings only the particu-lar insights needed to complement his own work. And yet the German post-war public could hardly have wished for a more insightful inter-preter of Mead. Comparing his interpretation with the caricatures of pragmatism offered by Marxist intellectuals such as Lukács and Horkheimer, one sees why American pragmatism become known in 1950s Germany , even in left-wing circles, through the work of Gehlen – a cultural conservative with ties to the Nazi regime.

Why was Gehlen so interested in Mead? The answer to this question is associated with a central feature of American pragmatism's philo-sophical programme: the attempt to overcome Descartes's rationalism by means of a naturalistic philosophy of action. In order to achieve this goal, the pragmatists undertook a reconstruction of German idealism and of Darwin's evolutionary theory. This is the goal Gehlen shared with Mead. In other words, common to Gehlen's 'elementary anthro-pology' and to Mead's social psychology is an attempt to overcome the Cartesian body–soul dualism by means of the category of 'action'. Before we proceed, however, some words are needed, I believe, to clarify Gehlen's intellectual project. By taking into consideration the findings of modern biological and ethnological research, Gehlen's 'ele-mentary anthropology' aims at offering an empirically grounded philo-sophical interpretation of 'human nature'. As such, the scientific status of his philosophical anthropology is unique: it occupies an intermedi-ary position between the natural sciences and a metaphysical philoso-phy. If there is something characteristic about this anthropology it is its fundamental principle: the human 'capacity for action', understood as the structural law of human life.[3] As Gehlen explains,

we can and shall demonstrate how the human being's determination for action is the pervasive structural law of all human functions and achieve-ments, and that this determination results unequivocally from the human being's physical organization: a life form that is physically so constituted is viable only as an acting life form; and the structural law of all human effectuations, from the somatic to the mental, is thereby given.[4]

From this perspective, the 'special position of man'[5] – the central topic of an 'empirical philosophy' oriented to the reconstruction of the fundamental structures of humanity – is to be accounted for by the structure of human action. Gehlen conceives of the human being as a 'deficient being'[6] able to compensate for her inherent deficiencies only through action. Human beings are not adapted to a particular environment, they are not specialized as all other animals are and they lack true instincts. It is only through the capacity for action – understood as the human need to transform the world – that such beings are able to survive. In short, the special position of humans in the natural kingdom is closely related to their impulse for action. This idea was first explored by Fichte and Hegel, and later by the American pragmatists. In this light, the fact that, as we noted before, 'pragma' is the Greek word for 'affair, practical matter' is not insignificant.[7] In fact, the fundamental category that links Gehlen's philosophical anthropology to Mead's social pragmatism, and therefore explains Gehlen's interest in Mead's work, is the category of 'action'.

There is, however, a crucial difference between Gehlen's and Mead's treatment of this category. While Mead's conception of action is thoroughly intersubjective, Gehlen's proposal, despite being critical of the Cartesian rationalist solipsism, remains entirely solipsistic. At the core of Gehlen's 'elementary anthropology' one finds the notion of *Erlebnis*, an irrational and emotional experience which includes consciousness. *Erlebnis* is an individual act. It is interesting to note that, in utter contrast to Mead's opinion, Gehlen explicitly uses the figure of Robinson Crusoe as an illustration of his 'solitary actor'. Referring to the fundamental model of his anthropology, he observes that

> it was advisable to adhere to the abstract model of an imaginary solitary
> human being, a Robinson Crusoe, for then all further-reaching questions
> concerning society, social life, even sex could, so to speak, be put aside,
> leaving behind only a note as a reminder of them.[8]

It should be clear from the passage above that Mead's intersubjective analysis of the self was not enough to change the individualistic premises of Gehlen's anthropology. Nevertheless, Gehlen draws upon Mead in a number of respects, the most important of them being the one related to his own anthropological theory of language. Language is, according to Gehlen's analysis, not only the model for action but also the fundamental model for both self-interaction and the interaction between the human being and the world. In Part 2 of *Man*, Gehlen discusses at great length the five conditions for the acquisition of language, which he designates as the 'roots of language':

1   'life of the sound';
2   'sound-motor communication with visual impressions';
3   'recognition' (which enables human beings to categorize and interrelate isolated objects);
4   the 'call' (by means of which impulses are externalized);
5   'sound gestures' (which had been considered as the sole root of language by Herder).

Gehlen argues that Mead's conception of 'play' brings additional light to the fourth root, the 'call'. The call is an expression of the internal state of being; it can be exercised in solitude, as a self-reflective act. In the 1950 edition of *Man*, Gehlen introduces Mead's analysis of 'play' as an alternative to the explanations which accounted for it either as 'disguised seriousness' or as the result of some special 'drive to play'. In Mead's explanation of the developmental stages of 'play' and 'game', as well as in his concept of role-taking, Gehlen finds the model he needs to account for this fourth root of language. 'Play', as conceived of by Mead, expresses the crucial human process whereby 'relieved' interests develop ('relief' being a basic ingredient in Gehlen's analysis), communicative imagination unfolds and rules are invented. When rules emerge, games, understood as systems of reciprocal obligations, arise.[9]

There is yet another respect in which Mead's work serves to complement Gehlen's anthropology, namely his theory of the genesis of the significant symbol. Gehlen examines the category of the 'symbolic' both in his model of action and in his theory of language. In fact, actions and language are conceived of as 'analogous' phenomena. Just like words, deeds have their origin in play. At first, playful actions and language are without purpose; in time, though, they grow more complex and conscious. In Gehlen's view, Mead convincingly shows that the social-psychological mechanism of 'taking the role of the other' is the 'fundamental means through which the self learns to distinguish and confront itself and thereby develops self-awareness'.[10] Mead's thesis that this capacity for 'objectifying oneself, becoming distanced from oneself, possessing oneself',[11] explains self-awareness as arising from the awareness of others is considered by Gehlen as being of 'great importance'.[12]

Gehlen's appropriation of Mead's social psychology, however, is not without problems. On the one hand, the pragmatists' emphasis on democracy as a way of life, as the ethical standard of collective life, is simply missing from Gehlen's account. Of course, this is far from being surprising since Gehlen's democratic credentials were dubious, owing to his links with the Nazis. But let us agree that to omit the democratic dimension of Mead's thinking, a truly transversal category, one which cuts across all layers of his theoretical system, is a serious misrepresentation of his ideas. I would go as far as to suggest that, if one does not take into account the democratic character of Mead's social theory, one fails to grasp its very rationale. On the other hand, Gehlen tends to ignore the thoroughly intersubjective character of Mead's thought. Again, this entails a considerable misrepresentation. As we have seen, Mead believes human sociality to be responsible for two crucial achievements: the ability to communicate and the capacity for reflective thought. Deliberation and reflection are the two constitutive features of Mead's notion of the self. While Gehlen does not ignore the communicative character of human conduct, he does oppose discussion and reflection to action. In other words, whereas for Mead human beings act on the basis of an intersubjective exchange of opinions, be it only with themselves, for Gehlen action is grounded upon unquestioned beliefs about the world. Gehlen's anthropology thus fails to acknowledge the intersubjective nature of human action, which Mead always emphasized.

One can see now how these two omissions relate to one another. By failing to acknowledge the intersubjective character of the act, Gehlen does not represent rationality as intrinsically dialogical and communicative. Hence he does not pursue the radical democratic implications, ethical and political, of this form of rationality. In sum, Gehlen's frame of interpretation – anti-democratic and culturally conservative – severely limits his ability to learn from Mead.

Jürgen Habermas

In post-war Germany, Gehlen's reading of Mead marks the beginning of a second productive encounter between American pragmatism and German thinkers. The first encounter, as we have seen before, had taken place in the second half of the nineteenth century. At that time the idealism of Hegel, Humboldt and Fichte first entered the American intellectual context, chiefly through the 'Metaphysical Club' – a conversational club formed in Cambridge, Massachusetts, by Peirce, James and others, in 1872.[13] The story of the reception of Mead's ideas in Germany is, so to speak, a part of the second episode of this German–American encounter. I say 'a part' because the ideas of other pragmatists, including James, Peirce and Dewey, had already been subject to scrutiny by German thinkers since the 1920s. Nevertheless, I would like to call my readers' attention to the following point. The relevance of the reception of Mead's ideas in post-war Germany stems from the fact that the intellectual current which, along with Darwinism, made the strongest impact on the first-generation pragmatists was a German one – namely German idealism. In this light, it is of added relevance to examine how German social thinkers tried to re-establish, in completely different social and political conditions, the intellectual connection between 'their' sources of German idealism and American pragmatism. A case in point is Jürgen Habermas (b. 1927), who recalls his university days in the early 1960s as follows:

> Encouraged by my friend Apel, I also studied Peirce, as well as Mead and Dewey. From the outset I viewed American pragmatism as the third productive reply to Hegel, after Marx and Kierkegaard, as the radical-democratic branch of Young-Hegelianism, so to speak. Ever since, I have relied on this American version of the philosophy of praxis when the problem arises of compensating the weaknesses of Marxism with respect to democratic theory.[14]

As this passage suggests, Habermas has been relying for a long time on the resources provided by American pragmatism. For our purposes, it is worth noting that Habermas sees Mead as the first author to have made the shift from the paradigm of consciousness to the paradigm of language. That is, Mead's communicative social theory is given the status of a classical account, comparable to the contributions of a Weber or a Durkheim. As we shall see, this process of 'canonization' took its toll in terms of the type of contributions Mead is supposed to be credited for.

In what follows I will examine Habermas's interpretation of Mead in two successive steps. Firstly, I wish to discuss Habermas's usage of Mead's social psychology to tackle the problem of 'social individualization', that is, the process by which, in modern societies, socially produced selves grow increasingly individualistic. Secondly, I want to discuss a question of more general import. This is the 'canonization' of Mead achieved in the two volumes of *The Theory of Communicative Action* (1981) – the single most influential interpretation of Mead's work outside the symbolic interaction tradition. Not only has this move by Habermas allowed symbolic interactionism, 'still fundamentally committed to subjective actors and a linguistic behaviourism, to enter into the discussions of social and sociological theory suitable to issues in a global, social world';[15] it has also paved the way for a reassessment of Mead's contributions to contemporary social and political theory.

Before we proceed, however, a brief description of Habermas's project might be of help. Habermas is the leading figure of the second generation of the Frankfurt school, a current of critical theory which is an 'heir . . . of German idealism'[16] and aims at transforming current, existing societies into an ideal 'society in which the "people" have become autonomous individuals choosing their government and determining their life'.[17] After the 1970s in particular, Habermas tried to found a critical theory of society no longer based upon epistemological grounds, but upon the reconstruction of the set of human communicative competences. In other words, his critical theory underwent a 'linguistic turn'. In this context, Mead's social psychology served Habermas as a guide towards a theory of communicative action that aims at connecting three different traditions: the critical theory of the Frankfurt school; the methodology of the hermeneutical tradition; and the dialogical conception of language and communication, initiated by Humboldt and developed, among many others, by Mead himself.[18]

Habermas's latest confrontation with Mead's ideas, in the pivotal essay *Postmetaphysical Thinking* (1988), revolves around the conceptual dilemma of providing a sociological explanation for a problem that Gehlen has ironically described as 'an individual – that's an institution in one instance'.[19] Sociology's account of individuation, from Durkheim to Parsons, is unsatisfactory because it does not distinguish properly between the processes of differentiation and those of individualization. The issue at stake here is that, in modern developed societies, there is a social process through which the self becomes, simultaneously, more individuated and more institutionalized. Gehlen's irony thus entails a criticism of modernity (similar to Foucault's) as an illusory project: the promise of liberation from social expectations and stereotypes is immediately contradicted by the description of this very promise as a new sort of normative expectation. Habermas's proposed solution for this paradox consists in recovering a far-reaching idea of Mead, according to which

> individuation is pictured not as the self-realization of an independently acting subject carried out in isolation and freedom but as a linguistically mediated process of socialization and the simultaneous constitution of a life-history that is conscious of itself.[20]

In Habermas's opinion, the relevance of Mead's contribution lies in the fact that he is the first social thinker to propose an entirely intersubjectivist model of the self. The relative advantage of such a model over the previous paradigm of consciousness is that it permits the conception of self-consciousness 'not as a phenomenon inherent in the subject but one that is communicatively generated'.[21] Equipped with Mead's theory of the self, sociologists now have the conceptual apparatus that enables them to explain how social actors are becoming increasingly individualistic and why this growing individualization becomes, in turn, an institution. Habermas's reading of Mead is as clever and ambitious as it is controversial.

According to Habermas, Mead's 'I–me' distinction, if adequately reconstructed, can provide a useful analytical tool to explain the emergence of what he calls 'post-conventional ego identities'. In pre-modern societies, selves were defined in terms of concrete networks of interaction. The societal trend towards differentiation, one of the features of modern social formations, has put an enormous pressure upon these 'conventional identities'. Habermas is referring, in particular, to a 'generalization of values and, especially in the system of rights, a universalization of norms'.[22] These processes have far-reaching consequences for identity formation. The modern self, like its pre-modern predecessor, can only be thought of as socially constituted. However, the 'social formation corresponding to it in any way does not yet exist'[23] – it has to be anticipated. Specifically, the post-conventional identities of our times can only stabilize themselves if they are able to anticipate 'symmetrical relations of unforced reciprocal recognition';[24] and the 'I' is supposed to be responsible for the projection of such communities of an unlimited communication. Treating Mead's distinction between the 'I' and the 'me' as historically contingent, Habermas claims that, in late modernity, the relationship between the two has been 'reversed':

> Previously, the 'me' was supposed to capture a spontaneously acting 'I', which eludes direct seizure, in a nonobjectifying manner, in mediated acts of self-knowledge or self-reassurance. Now, however, the anticipatory establishment of interactive relations to a circle of addressees is imputed to the 'I' itself . . . The 'I' itself *projects* the context of interaction that first makes the reconstruction of a shattered conventional identity possible on a higher level.[25]

Admittedly, this is a very cunning move by Habermas. In late modern societies, there is an increasing proportion of 'post-conventional' identities. By reversing Mead's duality, Habermas believes he is able to explain why such 'post-conventional' identities require individuals to anticipate an ideal community in which autonomy (moral sphere) and self-realization (ethical sphere) can be reconciled.

Habermas's accomplishment, however, is not without problems. Mead's 'me' is transformed into a purely conservative force, blindly subjugated to external social controls, whereas the 'I' is given the function of guaranteeing the continuity of one's life history. Distinguishing between an epistemic self-relation and a practical relation-to-self, Habermas suggests that the 'I' in this second capacity performs the function of a free will, of reassuring ourselves about ourselves. But in my view Mead's emphasis on the creative aspects of human action, one of his major potential contributions to contemporary social theory, is replaced by Habermas's own emphasis on the question of 'self-affirmation'. Moreover, whereas Mead asserts that the 'I' has primacy over the 'me', Habermas sees the latter as the 'bearer of a moral consciousness'.[26] In other words, Mead's 'I', with its capacity for unleashing creativity, originality and unpredictability, is a conceptual tool more attuned to the features of post-conventional personalities than Habermas's 'I', which is limited to the maintenance of one's identity over time. As Mead saw it, to be reassured of our uniqueness is not the only thing that matters; one has to be unique in relation to the community in which one lives.

Turning now to Habermas's discussion of Mead's contributions in *The Theory of Communicative Action*, I would like to begin by emphasizing the relevance of this two-volume work for the reception of Mead's ideas outside the US. Among sociologists, Mead was known until the early 1980s as the inspiring figure of symbolic interactionism, a theoretical current that emerged as Parsons' structural functionalism was losing its predominance. With the publication of Habermas's *The Theory of Communicative Action* in 1981, Mead's image in sociology changes dramatically. Mead is no longer simply the first of the symbolic interactionists; he is one of the discipline's founding fathers, to whom we owe the paradigm shift from purposive to communicative action. In this work, Habermas revisits a classical sociological theme. The 'unfinished project of modernity' is discussed from the point of view of the process of rationalization. Distinguishing the 'system' components of society (market economy and the state bureaucratic apparatus) from the 'lifeworld' (culture, society and personality), Habermas presents a great narrative authors are said to have contributed to a better understanding of the process of rationalization, both on the level of system and on that of the lifeworld, whose protagonists are Marx, Weber, Mead, Durkheim and Parsons. All these authors are said to have contributed to a better understanding of the process of rationalization on the level of both system and the lifeworld.

Habermas begins his reconstruction of Mead's social psychology by focusing on the phylogenetic account of the emergence of language. Mead uses the concept of 'conversation of gestures' as an evolutionary starting point, which leads first to signal language and then to propositionally differentiated speech. Human language proceeds from the signal languages – which in turn mark the transition from gesture-mediated to symbolically mediated interaction – to become the basis for normatively regulated action. But there are problems with this account. According to Habermas, Mead's distinction between symbolically mediated interaction on the one hand, linguistically mediated and normatively guided interaction on the other is not adequate. In order to solve this difficulty, Habermas resorts to Wittgenstein's concept of rule. His point is that the transition from gesture-mediated to symbolically mediated interaction involves the 'constitution of rule-governed behavior, of behavior that can be explained in terms of an orientation to meaning conventions'.[27] In Habermas's view, Mead does not give the same weight to the three prelinguistic roots of the illocutionary power of speech acts. True, he did realize that language was the primary mechanism of socialization (which is linked to the emergence of norms and identities) and of coordination of action (which is related to the world of perceptible and manipulable objects); but he failed to inquire into the possibility of normative solidarity. As Habermas explains, Mead 'focuses on language as a medium for action coordination and for socialization, while leaving it largely unanalysed as a medium for reaching understanding'.[28] Thus Habermas focuses on Mead's ontogenetic account of the origin of personal identities and of objective perception, arguably one of the most sophisticated readings of his treatment of the topic.[29] The outcome of this analysis is the critical remark that Mead 'is moving in a circle'.[30] To Habermas's mind, Mead tries to explain the phylogenetic transition from symbolically mediated to normatively guided interactions by resorting to a concept which figures only in his theory of ontogenesis, namely the 'generalized other'. It is in order to overcome this difficulty that Habermas then turns to Durkheim's theory of religion.

When Habermas returns to Mead some sixty pages later, his purpose is to assess the extent to which Mead's contribution in fact supplements Durkheim's proposals. If Durkheim throws light on the phylogenetic origins of what Habermas designates as the 'linguistification of the sacred', i.e. the transfer of the societal functions of cultural reproduction, social integration and socialization, from the religious realm, to the structures of communicative action, Mead provides the explanation for these evolutionary trends from the perspective of socially individuated human beings. In other words, Mead is the first author to acknowledge the societal trend that Habermas calls the 'communicative rationalization of the lifeworld'.[31] However, Habermas still has some reservations concerning Mead's approach. The first one relates to the formalist character of Mead's analysis of the societal processes comprised in the rationalization of the lifeworld. The second and more crucial reservation has to do with Mead's alleged 'idealism'. Habermas turns to functionalism to compensate for Mead's 'neglect of economics, warfare and the struggle for political power',[32] which was due to his 'idealistic' theoretical model.

In my view, this criticism holds true for Blumer's Mead, given the apoliticism of symbolic interactionism and its focus on micro-aspects of social relations. It is, however, an entirely different thing to accuse Mead himself of neglecting the processes of 'material reproduction of society'. As I have tried to show, despite the extraordinary empirical wealth of the symbolic interaction tradition, the fact remains that Blumer and his followers have offered only a partial interpretation of Mead. I would thus like to make two different claims. In the first place, it is not entirely clear to me on what grounds Habermas should feel entitled to criticize an author with respect to aims he never envisaged. Mead did not intend to produce a critical theory of society; his aim was to provide a social-psychological explanation for the development of the human self. Secondly, and more importantly, it is simply not true that Mead neglected the sphere of politics, morals and international relations. Mead not only wrote extensively on these subjects, but he was a committed citizen for most of his adult life in Chicago. As we shall see below, this facet of his life and work has only recently been given due appreciation.

Hans Joas

Mead's inclusion in the sociological canon, promoted at first by symbolic interactionism, received a decisive impulse from Habermas's critical examination of his ideas. Curiously enough, at around the same time that Jeffrey Alexander published his monumental four-volume *The Theoretical Logic in Sociology* without a single reference to Mead or to the pragmatists, a continental thinker felt the need to retrieve the contribution of one of the classical American pragmatists in order to construct a grand sociological theory. The early 1980s witnessed a sudden upsurge of great synthetic sociological treatises,[33] yet Mead only figured prominently in Habermas's proposal. This is a clear indication of the special relation between American pragmatism and many post-war German social theorists.

Apart from Habermas, there is only one social thinker whose work on Mead not only has made a significant impact on Mead scholarship, but has also made extensive use of Mead's ideas in contemporary debates. This is Hans Joas (b. 1948), one of Germany's leading social theorists and the author of what is probably, still today, the single best intellectual biography on Mead. Joas' interest in American pragmatism, especially in Mead's work, began in the 1960s. Very much like Habermas and Apel, Joas believes that this trend can supplement the shortfalls of Marxism and other German intellectual traditions. A case in point is his *Social Action and Human Nature* (1980), a book co-authored with Axel Honneth. In this work, Joas and Honneth discuss Mead's theory of intersubjectivity as a complement to the proposals of Arnold Gehlen and Helmut Plessner, the two major figures of the German tradition in philosophical anthropology. But it is with *G. H. Mead. A Contemporary Re-examination of his Thought* (1985) that Joas established himself as one of the foremost experts on Mead.

Joas sees Mead not only as a figure of 'great philosophical relevance and importance today', but also as a social thinker whose contributions can help sociology to 'connect itself once again to the impulses that at one time gave it vitality and certainty about its future'.[34] Such a statement, subscribed to nowadays by most practitioners in the social sciences, would have been considered an oddity until the early 1980s, at least for sociologists outside the US. A decisive reason for such a change in the appreciation of the relative merits of Mead's contribution to sociology is Joas' seminal re-examination of Mead's work in 1981. Combining rigorous archival research, which enables him to move beyond the partial understanding of Mead's *oeuvre* suggested by Blumer and the symbolic interactionists, with a painstaking philosophical analysis of Mead's conceptual apparatus, Joas provides a fresh image of his subject. Mead is no longer considered to be predominantly concerned with face-to-face symbolic interaction. Rather, Joas tries to show how his thinking evolved over time, from a naturalized Hegelianism and functionalist psychology to a social pragmatism whose chief concern was the relation between action and consciousness. Moreover, important aspects of Mead's work such as his theories of the constitution of the body image, of the physical object and of subjective temporality, which had been completely overlooked by symbolic interaction, are thoroughly analysed.[35] One of Joas' central claims is that German idealism exerts a noticeable influence upon American pragmatists, Mead being no exception. And I think that Joas has good reasons to make this claim. The factual evidence in support of his thesis is simply overwhelming. Hegel's influence over Mead's early thought is not an issue; but I believe that we should still discuss what can be learned today from that first German–American encounter. I will come back to this point in my final remarks.

Nevertheless, Joas' reconstruction of Mead's thinking is not without problems, too. One of the criticisms that can be levelled at his study is that it does not pay enough heed to Dewey's influence upon Mead.[36] This is particularly true of Joas' discussion of Mead's work in the 1920s. While it is certainly the case that Bergson and Whitehead played a major role in Mead's later 'metaphysical' writings, Dewey was nonetheless an intellectual reference for Mead up to the very end of his life. And there is yet another kind of objection that can be raised against Joas' interpretation. As I have already pointed out, this author undertakes a rigorous historical reconstruction of the various phases of development in Mead's thinking; but this reconstruction is, however, only partially achieved. To make this point clearer, let me compare his book with Gary Cook's more recent intellectual biography of Mead.[37] Cook's work is that of a historian. It carefully reconstructs the various contexts in which Mead lived and worked, and it offers a meticulous analysis of almost every single paper written by Mead. From the perspective of social theory, however, Cook's contribution is limited – it fails to discuss Mead's ideas in the context of their reception by later generations of social practitioners. By contrast, Joas' volume aims at both historical accuracy and theoretical relevance. As I have argued elsewhere,[38] Joas' book comprises two different parts. The first one offers a historically minded reconstruction of Mead's thinking, showing how his ideas evolved over time; the second opts for a thematic reconstruction. The limitations of such a strategy are evident. Only by combining a historical reconstruction with a thematic one can we grasp how Mead's philosophical system evolved. In other words, one has to identify Mead's main areas of interest (science, social psychology and politics) and then proceed with a historical reconstruction of all of them at once. In this way one is able to see, not only the development of Mead's ideas on each area, but also their interconnectedness. For example, the psychological mechanism of 'taking the role of the other', a crucial element of Mead's conceptual apparatus, can be seen operating in the attitude of the research scientist, in the attitude of the social actor (both from a phylogenetic and from an ontogenetic viewpoint), and in the attitude of the citizen.

This is not to suggest, however, that Joas' interpretation should be seen as a dated or flawed reading of Mead. On the contrary, his book remains compulsory reading for anyone interested in Mead. The chief reason is that he offers a fresh re-examination of certain facets of Mead's life and work, such as Mead's portrait as a 'radically democratic intellectual'. Beginning with Mead's formative experiences during his stay in Germany in the late 1880s, in particular 'the impression made on him by the social-democratic German labour movement',[39] Joas rightly points out that Mead's 'practical involvement in education and politics exercised a very great influence on his theoretical evolution'.[40] More recently, this insight, which received little or no attention from the symbolic interactionists, was pursued by Andrew Feffer in *The Chicago Pragmatists and American Progressivism* (1993). In this notable study, Feffer discusses the practical and theoretical aspects of Mead and Dewey's political involvement in the industrial and class conflicts in Chicago from the mid-1890s until World War I. In particular, Feffer is able to show that most of Mead's political thinking revolves around the notion of the producer's ethos and around a secularized version of a religious ideal of self-realization. In short, Feffer, following Joas' lead, has convincingly demonstrated that behind Mead's and Dewey's insistence on community, social reconstruction, cooperation and scientific evaluation of problems one finds a constellation of ideas in which the traditions of religious idealism and producer republicanism are pivotal.

Axel Honneth

I have been trying to show how a number of contemporary social thinkers have retrieved important contributions from Mead's work. Among the most promising of these contributions I would emphasize the radical democratic implications of his social-psychological theory as discussed by Joas, Feffer and others.[41] This contention seems to be corroborated by the work of the current 'leader' of the Frankfurt school,

Axel Honneth (b. 1949). Honneth, a former student of Habermas, has drawn extensively upon Mead's 'I–me' distinction in order to develop a concept of the person that can, along with 'reflections in social theory and a diagnosis of the present era', provide the philosophical foundation for the idea of making the 'struggle for recognition into the pre-scientific point of reference for critical social theory'.[42] In other words, Honneth's appropriation of Mead is motivated by the belief that the latter's social psychology offers a convincing analysis of the relation between personal individuation and intersubjective recognition. In the following passage, I will examine Honneth's appropriation of Mead's social psychology as a complement to Hegel's theory of recognition – as presented in both *The Fragmented World of the Social* (1990) and *The Struggles for Recognition* (1995).

Honneth's chief contention against the variant of critical theory proposed by Habermas is that it perpetrates a split between moral philosophy and the scientific analysis of the 'statements which refer concretely to the moral reactions and feelings of everyday interaction'.[43] By contrast, Honneth aims to endow social criticism with an empirical foothold, by connecting the level of justification of moral norms with the empirical analysis of moral motivations. Honneth's central reference is the theory of recognition developed by Hegel during his Jena period. It should thus come as no surprise that the connection between these two levels of analysis is to be performed by the concept of 'recognition', once this notion is reconstructed in a postmetaphysical way. It is exactly at this point that Honneth takes recourse to Mead. 'Even today', he writes, Mead's 'writings contain the most suitable means for reconstructing the intersubjectivist intuitions of the young Hegel within a postmetaphysical framework'.[44]

There are three conditions that Hegel's idea of 'making the struggle for recognition' must meet in order to become the starting point of a critical theory of society. Firstly, one has to analyse the most relevant contributions produced by contemporary social theory; secondly, one has to make a diagnosis of the present era; and, finally, one has to define a concept of the person which explains how individual claims to recognition are anchored in every social actor.[45] The need to meet this third condition explains why Honneth turns to Mead's theory of the self.

Honneth begins by suggesting that Mead's intersubjectivist account of the human self should be seen as a first step towards a naturalistic justification of Hegel's proposals.[46] The specific contribution made by Mead is his definition of the psychological mechanism that explains how self-consciousness develops through the perception of the other. In Honneth's view, Mead's theory provides a naturalistic translation of the two types of relation to the self Hegel was concerned with: the 'practical relation-to-self', which refers to the normative understanding of ourselves as moral agents; and the 'epistemic self-relation', which refers to the cognitive relations by which one acquires self-consciousness. Given Honneth's interest in moral theory, it should not be difficult to understand why he focuses next on Mead's analysis of the ontogenetic development of the practical self-image. Now Mead explains how a child learns the elementary forms of moral judgement by means of the two phases of childhood development, 'play' and 'game', and I have discussed earlier how the notion of the 'generalized other' performs the function of assisting the transition between these two phases. A child becomes a social member insofar as it is able to take the role and the attitude of the organized social group, which thus becomes the 'generalized other'. In a clever move, Honneth observes that, if Mead's insight is correct, then it 'makes sense to use the concept of "recognition" for this intersubjective relationship'.[47] Compared with the three relations of recognition identified by Hegel – love, right and solidarity – Honneth argues that Mead's conception of the 'generalized other' represents 'not only a theoretical amendment but also a substantive deepening' of the legal recognition.[48] Mead's achievement lies in having been able to explain, through the perspective of the 'generalized other', how individuals recognize one another as legal persons. Or, as Honneth puts it,

> once partners to interaction all take on the normative perspective of the 'generalized other', they know – reciprocally – what obligations they have to each other. Accordingly, they can also conceive of themselves as bearers of individual claims, claims that the other knows he or she is normatively obliged to meet.[49]

Of course, the reconstruction of the formative process of moral agents requires not only a reference to the 'me', but also to the 'I'. In the process of practical identity-formation, the impulsive 'I' is responsible for the reactions to social norms internalized by means of the 'me'. In Mead's words, '[o]ver against the "me" is the "I". The individual not only has rights, but he has duties; he is not only a citizen, a member of the community, but he is one who reacts to his community.'[50] Moral conflicts are then explained as outcomes of the inner tension between the 'I', with its claims to individuality, and the 'me', the bearer of the collective will inside one's self. Mead places great store by these demands of an individual's 'I' in the very process of societal development. As civilization unfolds, the demands of one's 'I' forces us to anticipate a future community in which larger freedoms would be accepted. As such, the 'generalized other' of our present community gives way to a future enlarged community of rights. Honneth believes this thesis to be in accordance with the Hegelian idea of a 'struggle for recognition', with one crucial advantage: Mead's social psychology 'reveals its motivational basis'.[51]

In contrast to Hegel, however, Mead's analysis of the mutual relations of recognition covers neither the love relationship, nor the solidarity relationship. In Honneth's view, this does not mean that one cannot
find in Mead's social psychology insights similar to Hegel's ethical
relationship of mutual recognition. In fact, Mead's concept of the 'generalized other', insofar as it 'identifies a relationship of mutual recognition in which every individual can know himself or herself to be
confirmed as a person who is distinct from all others in virtue of his or
her particular traits or abilities',[52] performs a similar function to Hegel's
Sittlichkeit (ethical life). While Mead does not offer an extended discussion on the mutual recognition of the individual's particular abilities,
his allusions to self-realization by means of socially useful labour do
represent, in Honneth's perspective, a 'post-traditional answer to the
Hegelian problem of ethical life'.[53] In sum, despite being excessively
objectivistic, Mead's model of the functional division of labour supplements Hegel's notion of 'solidarity' with the necessary 'motivating
experiential nexus'.[54]

It is now clear that the chief reason for Honneth's interest in Mead's
social psychology is the latter's ability to clarify the motivational foundations of personal autonomy in an intersubjectivistic manner. Up to
this point, I have no major reservations concerning Honneth's appropriation of Mead. For me the problem arises when Honneth suggests,
in *The Fragmented World of the Social*, that Mead's explanation of the
'genetic relation between personal individuation and intersubjective
recognition' offers no account of the universal 'motivational driving
force'[55] which turns individual claims to recognition into 'human
needs'. He then goes on to argue that we need to turn to psychoanalysis
in order to supplement Mead's social theory of the self. My reservation
concerns Honneth's suggestion that Mead's 'I' should be equated with
Freud's 'unconscious'. Assuming that Mead's 'I' is 'hardly different
from the unconscious in psychoanalysis', Honneth believes he can
describe Mead's account of individualization as the product of the
inner tension between the 'unconscious surge and conscious, linguistically mediated experience'.[56] But, as I see it, there are at least two crucial
differences separating Mead's notion of the 'I' from the concept of the
'unconscious' in psychoanalysis. On the one hand, Freud's tripartite
model of the mind (which includes the 'id', the 'ego' and the 'super-
ego') contains no functional equivalent to Mead's 'I', understood as a
phase of conduct that knows but is unknowable; on the other hand,
unlike Freud's 'unconscious', Mead's 'I' is sensitive to historical change
– as society evolves, so does the human self, including its impulsive
component.

In the paper 'The Potential and the Actual: Mead, Honneth, and the
"I"', Patchen Markell has recently discussed Honneth's appropriation
of Mead's 'I–me' distinction.[57] Combining a closely argued reconstruction of the development of the 'I–me' distinction in the course of Mead's

career with a philosophical analysis of Honneth's account of recognition, Markell certainly offers the best commentary available on the topic. What is noteworthy in Markell's paper for our purposes is the innovative reading of Mead's 'I–me' distinction he offers. Markell, whose interests are in ethical and political theory, suggests that in some passages the 'I' is described by Mead not as a source of creativity or spontaneity within the self, but as something 'which is actually going on, taking place'.[58] In his view, Mead's shifting use of the term 'I' has far-reaching implications for moral philosophy. If Markell is right, then the 'I' should not be represented as a source of potentiality which must be actualized through recognition (this happens to be Honneth's claim), but rather as action, as an 'actual response'. In more general terms, Markell believes that Mead's model of the self can provide us with the conceptual tools needed to overcome the dualism separating 'potentiality' from 'actuality'. If one renounces this dualism, one no longer runs the risk of justifying or reinforcing, even if unwillingly, the hierarchical division between the rulers and the ruled: for most rulers justify their dominion over others precisely on the strength of their authoritative assessments of the potentialities of the ruled. And this would be the chief limitation of Honneth's model of recognition. As Markell forcefully puts it,

> even the most expansive, egalitarian grant of recognition will remain just that: a *grant*, performed by already-privileged agents whose authority is not in question, its egalitarianism framed and partially betrayed by a certain structure of condescension.[59]

It is exactly this limitation that Mead's 'I–me' distinction would be able to help us to overcome. So both Honneth and Markell find in Mead a powerful ally in answering one of moral philosophy's most intractable problems: How can one resist injustice? Honneth opts for recovering Hegel's model of recognition, supplementing it with Mead's social psychology, and then complementing Mead's theories with a psychoanalytical concept of human identity. By contrast, Markell does not find it necessary to transform Mead's 'I' into Freud's 'unconscious'. He simply reads Mead in his own pragmatist terms, avoiding rigid dichotomies such as the one between the 'potential' and the 'actual'. I find that Markell's option is sounder. If Mead is to inspire us to solve our problems, he must be read on his own terms. This does not mean, of course, that we should not be creative in trying to find our own answers. Markell's work is a good example of what I have in mind.

American sociology today

Interesting and informed as it may be, Markell's recent appropriation of Mead lies beyond the disciplinary boundaries of sociology. If one wishes to dwell on the usage of Mead's ideas by contemporary sociologists one must look elsewhere. In the remainder of this chapter, I will discuss the cases of two prominent American sociologists who have, in one way or another, tried to make use of Mead's legacy. In the 1980s and 1990s, Randall Collins (b. 1941) and Jeffrey Alexander (b. 1947) attempted to come to grips with the sociological import of American pragmatism in general and of Mead's social psychology in particular. Collins had no hesitation to claim, in his well-known article 'Toward a Neo-Meadian Sociology of Mind' (1989), that Mead 'is no doubt America's greatest sociological theorist'.[60] But before I discuss Collins' appropriation of Mead's ideas, some words to clarify his theoretical agenda are in order, since Collins gained prominence in the 1970s as one of the main figures of conflict theory.[61]

Collins' version of conflict theory distinguishes itself from others (e.g. that of Ralf Dahrendorf) by drawing not only on the writings of Marx, the sociological classic most closely associated with conflict theory, but also on a myriad of other sources, including Weber, Durkheim, Schutz, Goffman and Mead. It still exhibits all the major features of conflict theory: society is conceived of as a realm where social groups compete for various kinds of resources, individual action is driven by interests and ideas are resources that can be mobilized in social conflicts. Actors, Collins suggests, have a set of basic interests or 'goods' they will pursue wherever they happen to live. The most important of these social goods are wealth, power and prestige. Furthermore, social conflict is an endemic characteristic of human societies because these goods are 'inherently scarce commodities'.[62] Following Weber, Collins argues that social life can be understood as comprising three main areas within which social agents compete for resources, thereby creating patterns of social stratification. Firstly, the sphere of occupations is related to the grouping of individuals according to social classes; secondly, the communities where individuals live determine their grouping according to status groups, which can be based upon attributes such as gender, age, ethnic origin and educational abilities; thirdly, the realm of politics is organized according to ideological cleavages which, in turn, give origin to political parties that seek to maximize their influence and power.[63] Collins has applied this general analytical framework to a number of specific cases.

A good example can be found in his analysis of higher education, one of his most accomplished pieces of empirical sociological research.[64] To put it briefly, Collins shows that the extensive periods dedicated to higher education in industrial societies perform an important, though often ignored, social function. Rather than merely providing the skills necessary for the occupations characteristic of our age (job skills are learned in the workplace, not in universities), Collins suggests that educational credentials perform a 'gatekeeping' function. Most educational credentials for a job – say, the professional jargon – have no obvious relevance to the performance of the post in question, but constitute a crucially important element in limiting access to it.[65] Collins' educational elite of contemporary societies acts very much like the Chinese literati described by Weber: both groups use education as a means to monopolize access to prestigious, well-paid and influential occupations. Hence the 'credential inflation' which developed societies have been experiencing in the past few decades: the more the educational elite set up job entry requirements that favour themselves, the more people are willing to invest in educational credentials, and the more employers have to raise entry requirements to face the increasing number of applicants. The image of education that emerges from Collins' conflict theory is a far cry from the commonly held view of education as a socially neutral, merit-based provider of the occupational abilities demanded by the job market; much to the contrary, Collins is able to show that education should be seen as one of the most important bases of status-group differences.

Now in my judgement Collins' analysis of Mead is far from being successful, although it has to be acknowledged that his is one of the very few attempts by a contemporary American sociological theorist to incorporate insights from Mead. What is Collins' goal? In his own words, he aims at a 'sociological theory of who will think what kinds of thoughts under what conditions', which he would reach by filling out Mead's social theory of the self with 'Durkheimian/Goffmanian/ conflict theory lines of analysis'.[66] The goal of creating a 'sociology of mind', which should explain how social interaction, dialogue and thinking are related to each other is certainly commendable. Numerous symbolic interactionists have drawn upon Mead's social psychology in order to shed light on this very area of social life – and, I might add, with success. But, if Collins' goal of building a theory of 'interaction ritual chains'[67] is praiseworthy, the same cannot be said of the way he appropriates Mead's ideas to achieve (and illustrate) that goal.

Consider first of all Collins' critical remark that Mead's behaviourism is a 'vulgar' behaviourism, characterized by anti-intellectualism, a crude utilitarian pragmatism and a simplistic drive-reduction model.[68] It is upon this foundation that Collins bases his claim that the 'crucial respect in which Mead's behaviorism is lacking is its failure to include sociability as a human end in itself. . . . His world actually seems to consist of isolated individuals, pursuing their own, rather mundane physical activities'.[69] Even to the most sympathetic reader, such a claim is nothing less than a serious misunderstanding of Mead's work. Collins fails to see the central, constitutive component of Mead's social theory of the self; sociality is the axis around which his account of symbolically mediated interaction revolves. Human action is, as we have seen, as much oriented toward physical objects as it is towards social ones.

Collins' failure has two implications. Firstly, his argument for combining Mead with Durkheim – who is supposed to complement Mead's crude utilitarianism – becomes groundless. Secondly and crucially – given that Collins employs his 'neo-Meadian' theory to explain Mead himself – such a misleading interpretation is not exactly the most auspicious illustration of his own theory of interaction ritual chains. Collins' monumental *The Sociology of Philosophies* (1987) – a sweeping sociological analysis of the inner structure and process of development of every major philosophical tradition in the past two millennia – attempts to explain sociologically the 'thinking of intellectuals'. Albeit convincingly pursued in some cases, this idea is less successful when it comes to Mead. Collins' sociology of mind is a far less reliable interpretative instrument than the historical accounts provided by Mead scholars such as Joas, Cook or Feffer. To interpret a sociological classic such as Mead is a matter of historical rigour as much as of insightful understanding; but on both these accounts Collins' work cannot be said to equal the available alternatives in Meadian scholarship.

Be that as it may; fortunately Collins' appropriation of Mead's ideas did not end here. In *Interaction Ritual Chains* (2004), one of the most original and ambitious books on social theory in the past few years, Collins returns once more to Mead for inspiration. His central contention is that from the 'dynamics of situations' we can 'derive almost everything that we want to know about individuals, as a moving precipitate across situations'.[70] Drawing on Durkheim's analysis of the sacred and on Goffman's work on interaction ritual, Collins argues that face-to-face interactions should be conceived of as the basic social mechanisms; in his view, these 'interaction rituals' (IRs) give rise to shared emotional energy and symbolic meanings, which individuals then transport into what Collins calls 'chains' of interaction rituals. In his view, these chains – very much like Durkheim's tribal rituals, which give origin to a sense of collective effervescence and to a sense of group identity – are responsible for ritual outcomes such as group solidarity, emotional energy (EE), sacred objects and standards of morality. Of course, as in any other ritual, there are certain 'ingredients' that these IRs must contain in order to be successful: bodily co-presence, barrier to outsiders, mutual focus of attention and shared mood.[71] According to Collins, the crucial ritual ingredient is the creation of a mutual focus of attention, which is, in turn, closely associated with the most important ritual outcome, emotional energy. As he puts it:

> This is above all what rituals do: by shaping assembly, boundaries to outside, the physical arrangement of the place, by choreographing actions and directing attention to common targets, the ritual focuses everyone's attention on the same thing and makes each one aware that they are doing so.[72]

If what rituals do is to focus every individual actor's attention on the same thing, their chief outcome is to produce emotional energy. This is particularly important, Collins contends, because human actors are above all 'emotional energy seekers' – that is, we are all driven by desires, the wish to be famous and dominant and the quest for excitement. This is what defines human beings: 'If not EE seekers, what else could human beings be?', asks Collins.[73] Behind this conception of the self, one finds Mead's notion of the 'I'. In a chapter entitled 'Internalized Symbols and the Social Process of Thinking', Collins draws heavily upon Mead's theory of the self, and specifically upon Mead's 'I–me' distinction. He equates the 'I', Mead's designation for the impulsive phase of the self, with emotional energy. In his own words, 'one's "I" is called forth in varying strengths by present interactions and past symbolic residues, magnetically attracted to some situations and repelled by others'.[74] For our purposes, it is noteworthy that one of Mead's conceptual elements has been given centre stage by one of the foremost sociological theorists currently working in the US. Indeed, by defining his theory's central concept in terms of Mead's 'I', Collins is setting a precedent for other leading contemporary theorists.

And now I would like to turn my attention to one of these theorists, Jeffrey Alexander – another American sociologist who has been recently drawing upon Mead's work. As with Collins, however, Alexander's interest in Mead's ideas is a subsidiary element of his theoretical agenda. Alexander's central concern is to create an original sociological theory, building upon the structural functionalism of Talcott Parsons as well as upon other strands of classical and contemporary sociological theories. In fact, until recently Alexander did not pay much attention to American pragmatism – an option already chosen by Parsons, his intellectual mentor: neither in Parsons' 1937 *Structure of Social Action* nor in Alexander's 1981–3 *Theoretical Logic in Sociology* can one find a single reference to the contributions made by the pragmatists to sociology. It is only in 1987, with the publication of *Twenty Lectures*, a compilation of his lectures on American sociological theory in the post-war period, that Alexander finally breaks his silence on Mead and the pragmatists.[75]

Alexander devotes a whole third of his *Twenty Lectures* to Parsons. In a way this is understandable, given that this book picks up the thread from the end of Alexander's previous book. While *The Theoretical Logic* covers the classical sociological theories of Marx, Weber, Durkheim and Parsons, *Twenty Lectures* begins with Parsons (now considered a 'classic') and ends with contemporary theories such as symbolic interactionism, phenomenology and dramaturgical theory, ethnomethodology, cultural theory and critical theory. Apart from the glaring absences of central sociological theorists such as Giddens, Bourdieu or Luhmann, there is one further point of contention in

Alexander's account. The author proposes to evaluate his gallery of theorists in terms of their treatment of two allegedly central presuppositions of sociology: the problem of order and the problem of action. It so happens, however, that Alexander fails to justify these presuppositions. They are merely proclaimed to be the two central sociological concerns, but no attempt is made to demonstrate that the social thinkers in question ever shared them. Hence the disparate achievements of Alexander's analyses – quite convincing in what refers to Parsons but less so when applied to critical theory, ethnomethodology and symbolic interactionism. Yet it has to be said that Alexander's reading of Mead is both balanced and accurate.

Alexander's Mead is, namely, an author whose orientation towards collective and institutional issues has not been adequately recognized by Blumer – criticized here for being an 'individualistic' thinker. Had this not happened, Mead's 'early theory of interaction' could have made a 'considerable contribution to theoretical debate in the post-Parsons period', claims Alexander.[76] Symbolic interactionists are thus depicted as a group of sociological thinkers who have misinterpreted Mead's otherwise relevant contributions to contemporary social theory. Hence it is necessary to reconstruct Mead's legacy in a way that respects his collective thrust. This is exactly what Alexander proposes to do, especially with regard to Mead's notion of the 'generalized other'. This can be seen in the 1998 'After Neofunctionalism: Action, Culture, and Civil Society', a paper where Alexander discusses his own 'neofunctionalist' research programme by reference to what he has called 'the new theoretical movement'. This expression is meant to describe a broad tendency among contemporary sociological theorists to advance proposals for general, synthetic theories. Representatives of this new theoretical movement include, apart from Alexander himself, authors like Habermas, Niklas Luhmann, Richard Munch, Anthony Giddens, Pierre Bourdieu, Luc Boltanski and Laurent Thévenot and Randall Collins. Alexander's neofunctionalism is, from this perspective, an attempt to build upon some of Parsons' basic ideas while 'criticizing his theories in fundamental ways'.[77] This ambition, of creating a synthetic sociological theory by combining Parsons' ideas with those of many other social thinkers, including Mead, is the chief distinctive feature of Alexander's current theoretical agenda.

This agenda comprises three main areas in which he is moving beyond the theoretical reconstruction of Parsons' legacy to theory building. That Alexander is still very much under the influence of structural functionalism is clear judging from his adoption of Parsons' 'three-system model', which includes the personality system, the cultural system and the social system. Action, culture and civil society are thus Alexander's favoured research areas. As far as 'action' is concerned, I think Alexander is right when he emphasizes the need to distinguish between 'agency' and 'the social actor'. While the former refers to a dimension of action which does not depend on constraints (either internal or external), the latter refers to the concrete persons who exercise agency: 'Action, then, is the exercise of agency by persons',[78] as Alexander forcefully puts it. One obvious advantage of such a distinction is that it helps to avoid the reproduction of the all too familiar dichotomy between the individual actor and the social structure. When one identifies agency with social actors, one is actually reproducing the old dichotomy in another form. Actors and structures, instead of being separated hierarchically, are simply put side by side. On the one side, we have the actors as the locus of agency; on the other, we have the structures as the locus of constraints to action. Alexander brings two to make his point. The early philosophical anthropology of Joas and Honneth locates creativity only at the individual level, thus neglecting its association with 'dimensions of culture and social structure that can be vital resources in the construction of the capacities and identities of actors themselves'.[79] Collins, however, equates structure with material, impersonal resources such as power or property and conceives of agency as being generated by internal and emotional responses to the external environment.

On this matter at least, Alexander's proposal is remarkably similar to Mead's insights. As we have seen, Mead conceives of the 'I' and the 'me' as two phases of the self, which in turn is but a phase of a larger social process. The self is, therefore, a social self insofar as it is part and parcel of the ongoing social experience. Alexander seems to reproduce this processual view of the relationship between individual actors and social structure when he claims that '[c]ulture and personality are themselves social structures, forces that confront agency from within and become part of action in a "voluntary" way'.[80] Of course, Alexander is not merely reproducing Mead's view; he should be credited for putting forth a fresh and powerful meta-theoretical claim, which happens to be consonant with Mead's process view of society.

Regarding culture, Alexander makes a very simple yet strong claim: culture has to be conceived of as an 'organized structure internal to the actor in a concrete sense'.[81] To do otherwise is to make the mistake of equating culture with structural patterns that always remain external to the individual, a mistake which results from failing to distinguish action from agency. The aim of Alexander's 'strong program of cultural sociology'[82] is to overcome a difficulty faced by cultural sociologists and general theorists alike: 'their approach to agency', Alexander contends, 'is not only conflationary but celebratory and even heroic'. One of the examples he provides is the symbolic interactionists' conception of actors as 'endlessly creative, expressive, and meaning-making'.[83] Fortunately, claims Alexander, with the development of the 'new theoretical movement' towards synthetic proposals, symbolic interaction is moving beyond Blumer's 'emphasis on individualistic contingency'.[84] Reiterating a point already made in *Twenty Lectures*, Alexander then argues that this movement will only be successful if symbolic interactionists realize the potential of Mead's 'collective thrust',[85] a crucial resource for contemporary social theory.

And yet I have not touched upon Alexander's most explicit claim about Mead's contributions, which concerns the world of 'civil society' and the civil sphere. In particular, he frames his appropriation of Mead's ideas within an important meta-theoretical claim. The 'informal social order' suggested by the work of symbolic interactionists such as Blumer or Goffman has been one of the inspiring motifs of many general sociological theories in the 1980s and 1990s. However, as the examples of Habermas's theory of communicative action or Collins' conflict theory indicate, these contemporary theorists have not achieved more than to 'synthesize microsociological models of interaction with the conflict-oriented structuralism'[86] associated with the neo-Weberian and neo-Marxist proposals of the 1960s. As such, they are not able to supersede the limitations of the old dichotomy between universalism and particularism. Focusing on the category of 'civil society', one of the most hotly debated political notions of the 1990s, Alexander argues that, in order to overcome the one-sidedness of such proposals, one needs to adopt a 'more concrete, empirical approach to action' which, in turn, will contribute further to the 'process of creating a new theory of civil society'.[87] It is at this point that Alexander brings in Mead's contributions, alongside the ideas of Simmel, Goffman and Boudon, referring to them as 'important descriptions of the distinctively interactional level of a civil order'.[88] In particular, Mead's concept of the 'generalized other' is said to be relevant for a better understanding of the way spontaneous cooperation occurs at the civil level. One can now see how Alexander's new synthetic theory, which draws on Parsons' work yet tries to go beyond it, is also indebted to Mead's ideas. This is, however, a declaration of intentions more than a cogent demonstration of how one can apply Mead's theories to the analysis of contemporary social problems: the reference to his ideas is presented towards the end of Alexander's paper, and none of Alexander's subsequent publications has so far pursued this promising line of inquiry.[89]

In sum, both Alexander and Collins have found in Mead a source of inspiration for their sociological theories. This reinforces the idea that Mead's social psychology can indeed be of use for contemporary sociology. In contrast to the theories of Habermas and Joas, however, neither Alexander's neofunctionalism nor Collins' theory of IR chains revolves around Mead's insights. For these two leading American sociological theorists, Mead is a secondary figure. While Parsons is still Alexander's chief intellectual reference, Collins has been trying to combine Durkheimian and Goffmanian ideas in order to produce a general sociological theory. In either case, the sociological import of Mead's social pragmatism is yet to be explored to its full potential.

As I have tried to show, the only sociological tradition that has selected Mead as its central intellectual source of inspiration is symbolic interactionism. From Blumer to Becker and Strauss, symbolic interactionists have built up an empirically oriented sociological alternative to Parsons' structural functionalism. Still, it should by now be clear that this appropriation of Mead's ideas has been highly selective, leaving behind crucial dimensions of his work.

The influence of Mead's ideas has also been felt outside America, most notably in post-war Germany. Through the work of cultural conservatives such as Gehlen or critical theorists such as Habermas, Honneth and Joas, generations of continental social scientists have been introduced to Mead. This cross-Atlantic dialogue has been of enormous fertility. Among continental social scientists and philosophers, the image of Mead as a 'seminal thinker of the very first order' is a result of the work of symbolic interactionists as much as of the German thinkers mentioned above. Contemporary sociologists on both sides of the Atlantic, keep returning to Mead in search for insights into new problems. This must be the surest sign of the continuing relevance of Mead's ideas. In the following chapter I will elaborate on this thought by trying to answer the question: 'Why should we read Mead today?'

8

Why Read Mead Today?

Of the sociological classics, none subscribes as wholeheartedly as Mead to a process view of the relationship between the individual and the collectivity. One of the most fashionable expressions in contemporary sociology – 'structure as process' – acquires in Mead a resonance that is simultaneously more authentic and more coherent than many contemporary proposals. It is more authentic because, as I have tried to demonstrate, the naturalized version of Hegel's dialectical method is one of Mead's earliest and most enduring intellectual references. It is also more coherent because Mead pursued more thoroughly than most the implications of his process view of reality.

For Mead, the guiding metaphor for social life is that of an ongoing experience, whose different phases are only intelligible insofar as they are conceived as part and parcel of a larger process. Of course, to translate this general philosophical insight into the theoretical discourse and methodological practice of today's sociology is not as obvious a move as it may seem at first sight. Mead, who was, after all, a social psychologist and never dreamt of becoming one of sociology's classics, was not concerned to provide an empirically verifiable sociological theory. In this chapter, my aim is to discuss the enduring relevance of Mead's ideas for contemporary sociology and social psychology. In particular, I wish to examine Mead's possible contributions to one of the most pressing problems in today's social theory: the extent to which the processes of 'identization'[1] and social reproduction depend on a conception of individual and collective creativity.

Mead, sociology and modernity

Admittedly, the theme of creativity is as old as philosophical reflection itself. Yet nowhere did creativity achieve such a prominence as in

American philosophy,[2] and especially in the writings of the American classic pragmatists.[3] The connection between creativity and modernity as a sociological theme has been recently rediscovered by a number of leading social theorists.[4] A reason for this recovery lies in the structural resemblances between what Peter Wagner calls the first and the second crises of Western modernity: while the end of the nineteenth century marks an epoch of crisis in the liberal model of modernity, a crisis that reaches its climax with World War I, the end of the twentieth century witnesses the crisis in state-organized modernity.[5] Not surprisingly, social sciences tend to reflect these societal trends. For our purposes, the disciplinary development of sociology is of particular importance: the high tide of sociology's modernist phase was reached in the 1960s (under the quasi-hegemonic influence of structural functionalism, systems theory and the associated quantitative–empirical methodologies), only to give way, first to the theoretical pluralism of the 1970s and later to the 'new theoretical movement' of the 1980s towards grand theoretical syntheses. One can then venture to suggest that what connects Mead's early liberal modernity to our late post-industrial modernity is a similar exposure to historical contingency, pluralism and hybridism. This is, in my view, the reason why the relation between creativity and cognition is as crucial a topic today as it was in Mead's time.

The 'progressive era' marks, in the context of the American variant of modernity, the passage from a liberal, individualistic and loosely organized social formation to a more coherently organized and collectively oriented historical period. As Mead's work attests, the role played by 'the social' has increased steadily from the late nineteenth century on, well into the first decades of the twentieth: the institutionalization of the social sciences and, in particular, pragmatism's debunking of rationalistic epistemologies and of methodological individualism are but symptoms of this general trend. The liberal model of modernity entered into crisis as soon as social and political practices, until then considered to be naturally self-regulating, began to demand the intervention of public authorities. The solution for this crisis required the state to mobilize specialized knowledge: only in this way could uncertainty be reduced, even if this meant incorporating it into the very theoretical instruments built to cope with it (as Mead's dialogue with Bergson and Whitehead so eloquently shows). In short, Mead's intellectual biography mirrors the historical period when uncertainties returned to shatter the then dominant liberal model. As the history of the city of Chicago at the turn of the century so clearly illustrates, rapid industrialization and urbanization paired with growing immigrant fluxes triggered a process of social change of enormous proportions; gone with it was the faith in a natural tendency towards certainty, order and coherence. One would have to wait for the end of World War II and for the rise of the welfare state to see a rebirth of these ideas, now in the form of a naturalized social order.

A few years after Mead's demise, Karl Mannheim, a sociologist of German origin who was to exert a pervasive influence upon later generations of sociologists, made a claim that would change the discipline's self-image. In *Ideology and Utopia* (1936), Mannheim suggested that there is a connection between the production of social knowledge and the social context in which that knowledge is produced: 'out of the investigation into the social determination of history arises sociology'.[6] From this moment on, sociology and modernity were conceived of as inextricably linked projects – an insight that Parsons, Marcuse and many others would later reinforce.[7] It was during the period of organized modernity (that is, from the late 1940s until the early 1970s) that sociology emerged as the modern science *par excellence*, i.e. a scientific discipline oriented to the study of the processes of modernization.

'Modernization theories', as they became known later on, consist of systemic and evolutionary accounts of social formations, whose change can be steered by nation-states. Societies, structured along clear lines of collective identity (class and national citizenship); the nation-state, a unitary political system whose sovereignty over a delimited territory was unquestioned; and sociology, developed so as to provide reliable empirical data and sound theorizing, were – so to speak – the three vertices of the triangle that constituted organized modernity. How can the state-organized phase of modernity be described? Within the physical boundaries set by national sovereign states, each and every individual had a clear social position and an associated 'role-set' (Merton). The notion of social integration is crucial to the understanding of the logic of this social formation. As the diffusion of modern features could be extended from the Western world to Third World countries, so, within developed countries, the material and symbolic benefits of modernity (the third generation of 'social rights' identified by T. H. Marshall[8]) could be extended to all national citizens.

Such is, in brief, the societal context in which the sociological debate on social roles was developed. This is a particularly important debate for our purposes since it connects Mead's ideas with the mainstream, modernist sociology of the 1960s. I am referring to Talcott Parsons, who tried to reconcile Mead's work with Ralph Linton's deterministic anthropology, in an attempt to link a theory of action and a theory of order. Parsons' functional–structuralist proposal did not, however, take sufficiently into account Mead's insistence on the connection between intersubjectivity and action. As a result, an overly deterministic portrait of social experience is suggested in Parsons' work: a social role is no more than the functional significance of individual action from the perspective of the social system.[9] Against the background of such a modernist sociology, with a distinct positivistic and behaviouristic bent, it is not difficult to see why it had to be a marginal theoretical current like symbolic interactionism that rediscovered the relevance of Mead's social-psychological theories for contemporary sociology. Mead's focus on the resolution of the problems resulting from the first crisis of Western modernity helps to explain why it was so difficult for the mainstream sociologists of the heyday of organized modernity to engage in dialogue with him.

In the late 1970s, a growing concern with the changing modes of constitution of individual and social identities could be discerned.[10] Postmodernism, a cultural movement that can be described as 'the modern mind taking a long, attentive and sober look at itself',[11] had begun its ascendancy in sociology and anthropology departments all over the Western world. There was a distinctively critical and pessimistic tone to this self-reflection on modernity's promises, achievements and shortcomings. Suddenly, a widespread sense of unease and scepticism emerged as to the possibilities of control, prediction and manageability of the societal project initiated centuries before. Postmodern social scientists increasingly adopted a distanced position concerning the 'great narratives' and 'collective actors' that the previous generation had learnt to see as embodying the historical evolution of the project of modernity.

As a matter of fact, this very notion of a single unified 'project of modernity' has been recently questioned by a number of scholars dissatisfied with the conflation between 'Westernization' and 'modernization' – a difficulty that can be traced back to the above-mentioned theories of modernization prevalent in the 1950s and 1960s, and even to the classical sociological analysis of Weber, Durkheim and Marx. The alternative perspective put forth by authors such as S. N. Eisenstadt or Göran Therborn emphasizes the existence of 'multiple modernities'.[12] In brief, this perspective suggests that, while it is the case that the first instance of modernity was 'deeply rooted in specific European civilizational premises and historical experience',[13] there has been ever since a continual reinterpretation of that programme in other parts of the globe. What is more, this encounter of Western modernity's themes and institutional forms with non-Western societies 'brought about far-reaching transformations in the premises, symbols, and institutions of modernity – with new problems arising as a consequence'.[14] Two main conclusions can be drawn from this perspective: firstly, Western modernity should no longer be considered to be the only 'authentic' modernity; secondly, the tendency to see the 'imbrications of modernity and tradition as exceptions, deviations'[15] should be discarded in favour of the notion that multiple modernities often are 'entangled modernities': the empirical history of modernity is far from linear, exhibiting numerous entanglements between the traditional and the modern. The existence of multiple and entangled modernities suggests an increased awareness of the fragile, contingent and changeable nature of the different projects of modernity. It is therefore not surprising that the relevance of Mead's contributions has become even more visible in this world of 'multiple modernities': Mead's insights can now be re-appropriated by non-Western audiences in the construction of their own variants of 'modernity'.

The past three decades have witnessed the growing erosion of most of the categories that characterized the state-organized phase of Western modernity: the nation-state is no longer the sole source of political legitimacy and sovereignty; societies are increasingly fluid (social norms are ever more subject to a denaturalization process); and individuals now face an overburden of possibilities of action that makes self-realization even more difficult. Contemporary societies are characterized by their growing differentiation, the acceleration of historical time and the concomitant compression of space, intense migratory fluxes and unprecedented technological advances. The proliferation of social roles, reference groups and social networks triggered by social experience in a globalized world determines the 'multiple bonds of belonging' described by Alberto Melucci: 'We have become migrant animals in the labyrinths of the metropolis, travellers of the planet, nomads of the present.'[16] The nomad, once considered the epitome of a bygone epoch, re-emerges today as a central sociological category; in order to understand the global 'tribes'[17] that cross the planet in search of entertainment, consumer goods and leisure it seems that one has to adopt a fluid, almost liquid perspective of modernity. In his rethinking of the concept of individuality around which the orthodox narrative of the human condition was written, Zygmunt Bauman observes: 'In a world in which deliberately unstable things are the raw building material of identities that are by necessity unstable, one needs to be constantly on the alert'; he then concludes that 'above all one needs to guard one's own flexibility and speed of readjustment to follow swiftly the changing patterns of the world "out there"'.[18]

That large-scale social changes are closely related to transformations at the level of the individual psyche should not come as a surprise to my reader, as Mead never ceased to emphasize the socially constituted nature of human subjectivity. Mead's radically social conception of the self thus seems to regain, at the dawn of the twenty-first century, an added significance. Ours is an age of uncertainty and indeterminacy.[19] To a certain extent, the same can be said of the 'progressive era' in which Mead lived. In both periods, modernity has been perceived as undergoing a time of crisis. It is my contention that, by reading an author whose work can be interpreted as an attempt to solve the epistemological and political problems posed by the first crisis of modernity, we can draw valuable lessons for coping with modernity's second crisis. In particular, the most important insight to be explored in Mead's work is his intersubjective conception of creativity, certainly one of the most promising theoretical resources available for dealing with the challenges posed by the current crisis of state-organized modernity.

In Mead, creativity is conceived as both cognitive and democratic: it expresses the human ability for reflective thinking and problem-solving and, as such, it is not limited to the figure of the 'artist' or the 'genius'. Every rational individual, argues Mead, is endowed with the ability to cope creatively with concrete action problems: the extent to which individual creativity is developed and refined is a question of personal development in as much as it depends on the kind of social experience one is exposed to. In turn, the degree of collective creativity a given community attains (expressed, for instance, in the quality of its artistic or scientific achievements) depends, as Mead puts it, on the actual scope offered for 'individuality – for original, unique, or creative thinking and behavior on the part of the individual self within it'.[20] For Mead, individual and social creativity are thus just two different phases of the same process by which original and innovative solutions are imagined so as to answer the problems individuals and groups face in everyday life. As an expression of reflective thinking, creativity is both a feature of the human species and a defining characteristic of modernity – the evolutionary stage of humankind in which the principles of rationality and individuality have attained their fullest expression.

During his long career of almost forty years, Mead aimed to solve the problem of reaching a socially sensitive account of the origins, process of development and internal structure of human subjectivity. Mead's proposed solution to this problem makes no concessions to Cartesian individualism – his is one of the most coherent versions of intersubjectivism produced in the twentieth century. It is perfectly understandable, then, that a growing number of social-psychological theorists in search of socially minded approaches to the self have been recently rediscovering Mead's work.[21] A similar trend can be detected among sociologists: Mead's process view of social life has received renewed attention ever since the early 1980s, approximately the same time when the sociological debate on the exhaustion of the project of modernity started to gain prominence. This is not to suggest that there is a connection between Mead's writings and postmodern concerns, even though some authors do point in this direction.[22] What I wish to contend, rather, is that there is a fundamental similarity between Mead's concerns and the problems that stand high on the current sociological agenda: the denaturalization of the process of formation of individual and collective identities, the epistemological problems concerning indeterminacy and the increased awareness of historical contingency are sociological issues as important today as they were a century ago.

In my view, reading Mead today offers us an extraordinary opportunity to learn to deal with the contingency that we all so profoundly experience in contemporary everyday life. To develop a social theory around the notion of creativity, which puts bio-social selves in a dialectical relation with social and cultural collectives, is as promising and urgent today as it was in Mead's time.

As I have tried to show, the omnipresent metaphor in Mead's *oeuvre* is that of a dialogue between rational individuals, a dialogue which is simultaneously at the origin of their rationality and their best option for solving the action problems posed by the surrounding environment. Mead's analysis of self-reflection is a convincing demonstration of the decisive importance of social cooperation and linguistic communication for the development of human rationality; as he used to point out to his students, the development of the cortex was only a necessary condition for the development of intelligence – without social experience there would be no minds. Robinson Crusoe's adventures on the island, far from illustrating the individual's ability to think and act in solitude, are instead a compelling example of the social nature of the self. In fact, even if Man Friday were to be discounted, Crusoe was never really alone on the island. As Mead has taught us, by the mere act of thinking, remembering and imagining, Crusoe was for the entire time a member of society, even if *in absentia*. Crusoe's mental life, a social product, was the link that bound him to the society he left behind and allowed him to cope successfully with the manifold cognitive action problems he was confronted with on the desert island.

Creativity, conceived of as a general feature of human beings; dialogue, understood as an ideal reference to human undertakings from science to politics; and human intelligence, viewed as a socio-linguistically human attribute, are thus some of the most important ideas around which Mead's thinking revolves. That he never gave his thoughts a final, fixed form should therefore not be surprising. Rather, this should be seen as an expression of the 'always in-the-making' nature of these thoughts. Mead's favoured medium for communicating his ideas was not the written word, but the uttered vocal gesture whose symbolic nature is a product of social life in as much as it is one of its conditions. In talking to his students and by deliberating with his peers, Mead has left us an immensely important legacy. It is now our responsibility to pursue all its implications for the resolution of the problems of our time.

How to read Mead?

So far, I have tried to provide an answer to the question: 'Why should Mead be read today?'; in what follows, I wish to answer a question as to 'how' that reading should be done. Thus, in order to help students with no prior knowledge of Mead to navigate through his writings, as well as through the most relevant secondary literature, this last section discusses the best way of entering this subject field. I will begin with Mead's published writings.

Until a new, complete edition of Mead's writings is published – an editorial project which, so far, has failed to attract the attention of an academic publisher – students and scholars alike have no option but to resort to the latest re-editions of the posthumously published books in the 1930s: *Mind, Self, and Society* (1934), *Movements of Thought in the Nineteenth Century* (1936), *The Philosophy of the Act* (1938) and *The Philosophy of the Present* (1932). For reasons detailed above, the editorial quality of these books is highly questionable: students should be made aware of this and encouraged to supplement their readings with other materials. Recently made available to the public by Mary Jo Deegan is *George Herbert Mead. Essays in Social Psychology* (2001), a book Mead prepared for publication in the early 1910s. In any case, I believe the best way of getting to know Mead's ideas is through the anthologies of his published articles: for instance, Andrew Reck's *Selected Writings. George Herbert Mead* (1964) provides reliable and comprehensive access to Mead's ideas. Also noteworthy is the online repository of Mead's writings, *George's Page*, which provides easy access to virtually all of Mead's published writings.[23]

I will now proceed with the presentation of the major interpretations of Mead's thought offered during the last decades of the twentieth century. As early as in 1971, Lewis Coser, with the assistance of Robert Merton, wrote *Masters of Sociological Thought*, which contains a chapter dedicated to a historically minded reconstruction of Mead's thought.[24] Soon after this, David L. Miller published what was at the time the most complete intellectual biography of Mead, with the explicit purpose of explaining his ideas in the light of the 1970s.[25] In 1980, Joas found in Mead 'the key to the desired convergence of two very different approaches of linguistic theory'.[26] By the 1990s, Andrew Feffer was following a contextualist method in his reconstruction of American pragmatism and of Mead's place in that movement,[27] while Gary Alan Cook saw himself as an intellectual historian.[28] These are our interlocutors in a debate organized around the question: How should we read Mead?

One of the first voices to make itself heard in trying to answer this question was that of Lewis Coser, much in the spirit of Merton's new history of science. In a demonstration of the effectiveness of the canonization process triggered by Blumer, Kuhn and other symbolic interactionists in the previous decade, Coser treats Mead on equal terms with Comte, Marx, Spencer, Durkheim, Simmel, Weber and others. Yet, confirming the effects of the partial appropriation of Mead's ideas by symbolic interactionism, Coser focuses only on one facet of Mead's work, his social-psychological theory. This said, Coser's account does include one of the first analyses of the contexts in the light of which the meaning of Mead's thought can be understood, therefore paving the way for historically accurate studies in the future. In fact, Coser was the first to denounce what he considered to be the myth of a unified 'Chicago school of sociology' in direct line of descent from Mead.[29]

A couple of years later, David L. Miller, a former student of Mead, published the most comprehensive study of his teacher's ideas to date. His purpose was to reconstruct Mead's system of thought, so that, in the future, Mead could be put in dialogue with authors such as White-head, Merleau-Ponty, Piaget, Husserl, Heidegger and the British ana-lytical philosophers.[30] Indeed, this extensive reconstruction deals with almost every aspect of Mead's intellectual edifice; but it faces a major difficulty. It assumes that Mead's system of thought can be recon-structed from the vantage point of his later writings, namely his prin-ciple of sociality.[31] Such an anachronism entails a reading of Mead's words which is at odds with his own intentions and insensitive to the evolution of his ideas over time. Therefore, Miller's answer to our ques-tion falls into a presentist reading of Mead's work.

In 1980, a new interlocutor joined this debate with what is certainly the most authoritative intellectual portrait of Mead to date.[32] Hans Joas avoided Miller's presentist reading and made extensive use of the Mead Papers archive. Yet his study is not merely a historical reconstruc-tion, for Mead is systematically discussed in the light of his contribu-tions to contemporary science, from ethics to epistemology and from social psychology to sociology. Joas distinguishes himself from all pre-vious commentators by asserting the need to take into account Mead's various fields of interest, even though he does not claim his account to be exhaustive.[33] Nevertheless, one can identify two different parts in Joas' book. In the first half, Mead's thought is reconstructed from the point of view of the evolution of his ideas, starting with a discussion of his personal biography and leading to a comprehensive study of the concept of 'symbolic interaction'. In the second half, Joas suddenly abandons this presentation strategy and systematically discusses various topics. Ethics, the constitution of the physical object, the theory of time and philosophy of science are the areas successively analysed. In terms of Joas' contribution to this debate, this inconsistency entails that his reconstruction of Mead meets its purposes only halfway. By reading Joas' account one can learn how some of Mead's ideas evolved over time and grasp the internal coherence of certain thematic areas. One cannot see, however, how Mead's system of thought evolved during the course of his career.[34]

Although Cook and Feffer share a contextualist methodological approach, their studies differ in a number of ways. Cook's study is in essence a historical reconstruction, particularly interested in discussing the genetic evolution of Mead's ideas in the light of the various settings in which he operated. In its own genre, Cook's study is a carefully argued and well-documented work. In my view, though, it can be criticized for assuming that the chronological presentation of one's ideas is tantamount to a critical assessment of one's thinking. The re-examination of an author's thinking requires not only the kind of historically minded analysis provided by a work such as Cook's, but also a rational reconstruction that allows for an evaluation of its systematic nature. To a certain extent, this is what Feffer tries to achieve. His study is guided by a concern to discuss the action and reflection of Mead, Dewey and other pragmatists from the point of view of their involvement in social reformist activities. This said, Feffer's account is somewhat limited by its exclusive focus on political issues.

All in all, though, there is no shortage of authoritative and stimulating commentary on Mead's ideas. In Mead, students will find a refreshing perspective on the social nature of the individual self. As I have tried to suggest, we now live in an era whose problems are remarkably similar to the issues that afflicted Mead's generation. His answers to the sociological and social-psychological problems of historical contingency, normative de-conventionalization and social fluidity are still today seminal insights worth pursuing. It is certainly not by accident that the 'linguistic turn' that has affected most of the human and social sciences in the past few decades, the 'deliberative turn' that dominates current political democratic thinking and the present general rejection of dichotomic theorizing are all so in tune with Mead's ideas. As social sciences and modernity(ies) evolve together, when a period comes which shares certain structural similarities with a past epoch, the writings of our predecessors suddenly gain an added relevance. This, I argue, is the case with Mead.

Notes

Chapter 1   Introduction and General Overview

1 By using the expression 'the heritage of sociology', I wish to pay homage to the University of Chicago book series of the same name, founded by the late Morris Janowitz.

2 The posthumously published anthologies of articles, *Selected Writings. George Herbert Mead*, ed. by Andrew Reck (Chicago: University of Chicago Press, 1964; repr. 1981); *George Herbert Mead. Essays on His Social Psychology*, ed. by John W. Petras (New York: Teachers College Press, 1968).

3 G. H. Mead, *Mind, Self, and Society from the Standpoint of a Social Behaviorist*, ed. Charles W. Morris (Chicago: University of Chicago Press, 1932; repr. 1997), p. 161.

4 Mead, *Mind, Self, and Society*, p. 191.

5 Donald N. Levine, *Visions of the Sociological Tradition* (Chicago: University of Chicago Press, 1995), p. 255.

6 Mead, *Movements of Thought in the Nineteenth-Century*, ed. Merritt H. Moore (Chicago: University of Chicago Press, 1936), pp. 144, 151.

7 Mead, 'Review of *Untersuchungen zur Phänomenologie und Ontologie des menschlichen Geistes* by Gustav Class', *American Journal of Theology*, 1 (1897).

8 Mead, 'A New Criticism of Hegelianism: Is It Valid? A Review of *Idealism and Theology: A Study of Presuppositions* by Charles F. D'Arcy', *American Journal of Theology*, 5 (1901).

9 Mead, 'A New Criticism of Hegelianism', p. 87.

10 Mead, 'A New Criticism of Hegelianism', p. 95.

11 Mead, 'Social Psychology as Counterpart to Physiological Psychology', *Psychological Bulletin*, 6 (1909), p. 406.

12 See Dewey, 'The Reflex Arc Concept in Psychology', in Jo Ann Boydston (ed.), *John Dewey. The Early Works, Volume 5: 1889–1892* (Carbondale: Southern Illinois University Press, 1972).

13 See Mead, 'Suggestions Towards a Theory of the Philosophical Disciplines', *Philosophical Review*, 9 (1900), p. 2.

14 The textual basis of this dialogue is Mead's 'The Definition of the Psychical', in *Decennial Publications of the University of Chicago*, First Series, 3 (Chicago: University of Chicago Press, 1903).
15 Mead, 'Definition', p. 91.
16 Mead, 'Definition', p. 109.
17 Hans Joas, *G. H. Mead. A Contemporary Re-examination of His Thought* (Cambridge, MA: MIT Press, 1985), p. 64.
18 Mead, *Mind, Self, and Society*, p. 13.
19 Mead, *Mind, Self, and Society*, pp. 2–3.
20 Joas, *G. H. Mead*, p. 6.
21 Mead, *Mind, Self, and Society*, p. 10.
22 Mead, *Mind, Self, and Society*, p. 6.
23 See Gary Cook, *George Herbert Mead. The Making of a Social Pragmatist* (Urbana, IL: University of Illinois Press, 1993), pp. 70–1. Joas had already called our attention to this issue: see Joas, *G. H. Mead*, p. 215, n. 6.
24 Mead, 'Review of *L'Evolution Créatrice* by Henri Bergson', *Psychological Bulletin*, 4 (1907), p. 384.
25 Mead, *Movements of Thought*, p. 325.
26 'The Objective Reality of Perspectives', in *Proceedings of the Sixth International Congress of Philosophy*, ed. Edgar S. Brightman (New York: Longmans and Green, 1926). This article was later included in *Philosophy of the Present*, ed. Arthur E. Murphy (La Salle, IL: Open Court, 1932; Amherst, NY: Prometheus Books, repr. 2002). I will quote from this later reprint.
27 See Mead, 'Objective Reality', p. 172.
28 Mead, 'Objective Reality', p. 173.
29 John Dewey, 'Prefatory Remarks', in *Philosophy of the Present*, ed. Arthur E. Murphy (La Salle, IL: Open Court, 1932; Amherst, NY: Prometheus Books, repr. 2002), p. 33.
30 John Dewey, 'George Herbert Mead', *Journal of Philosophy*, 28 (1931), p. 311.

Chapter 2   Life and Work: 1863–1931

1 Mead to his wife, January 31, 1895. Mead's letters, where this text comes from, are in the George Herbert Mead Papers, University of Chicago, Regenstein Library, Department of Special Collections. The other letters referred to in the subsequent notes come from *Henry Northrup Castle: Letters* (London: Sands, 1902).
2 *Henry Northrup Castle: Letters*, Mead, p. 807.
3 See Castle to his parents, November 4, 1882.
4 Mead to Castle, March 12, 1884.
5 D. N. Levine, *Visions of the Sociological Tradition* (Chicago: University of Chicago Press, 1995), p. 252.
6 Castle to Helen, October 9, 1887.
7 Mead to Castle, June 19, 1888.
8 I refer to Gary Alan Cook's discovery of Mead's infatuation with James' sister-in-law, Margaret Gibbens. James did not approve of this relationship and apparently asked Mead to cut short his tutoring work and to return to

Notes to pp. 20–25

Harvard. In this light, it is understandable that Mead decided to leave Cambridge, MA despite his earlier plans to study at Harvard. See Gary Cook, *George Herbert Mead. The Making of a Social Pragmatist* (Urbana, IL: University of Illinois Press, 1993), pp. 17–18.

9 The number of registered graduate students in American colleges and universities increased from 9,371 in 1870 to 34,178 in 1910. See Roscoe Hinkle, *Founding Theory of American Sociology 1881–1915* (London: Routledge, 1980), p. 36.

10 Donald Levine calls this process the 'University Movement'. By this he means the transformation in the 1880s of small liberal arts colleges into large research universities. See 'The Idea of the University, Take One: On the Genius of this Place', paper read at the 'Idea of the University Colloquium', University of Chicago, 8 November 2000, pp. 1–15.

11 Randall Collins, 'Toward a Neo-Meadian Sociology of Mind', in P. Hamilton (ed.), *George Herbert Mead: Critical Assessments*, 4 vols (London: Routledge, 1992), IV, p. 267.

12 Hinkle, *Founding Theory*, p. 44.

13 Castle to his parents, February 6, 1889.

14 Mead to Castle, n.d. (probably written at the end of 1890).

15 Mead to Castle, July 22, 1891.

16 Mead to Mr and Mrs Samuel Northrup Castle, June 18, 1892.

17 In which tens of thousands of workers went on strike to protest against low salaries and appalling work conditions.

18 Between 1918 and 1920, Mead served as president of this philanthropic organization.

19 This was a non-profit organization which provided social services for the most disadvantaged families living near the University.

20 See Philip Wiener, 'Pragmatism', in P. Wiener (ed.), *Dictionary of the History of Ideas*, 5 vols (New York: Charles Scribner's Sons, 1973), IV, p. 554.

21 Mead, 'A New Criticism of Hegelianism: Is It Valid?', A Review of *Idealism and Theology: A Study of Presuppositions* by Charles F. D'Arcy', *American Journal of Theology*, 5 (1901), p. 88. D'Arcy's book is an attempt to reconcile Hegel and Berkeley's analyses of human subjectivity.

22 Mead, 'A New Criticism', p. 89.

23 Mead, 'A New Criticism', p. 91.

24 Mead, 'A New Criticism', p. 95.

25 Mead, 'The Relation of Play to Education', *University of Chicago Record*, 1 (1896), p. 143. This article was originally presented as an address to the Chicago Commons in 1 May 1896.

26 Mead, 'Relation of Play to Education', p. 145.

27 Mead, 'The Working Hypothesis in Social Reform', *American Journal of Sociology*, 5 (1899), p. 367.

28 Mead, 'Review of *An Introduction to Comparative Psychology* by C. Lloyd Morgan', *Psychological Review*, 2 (1895); 'Review of *Du Rôle de l'Individu dans le Déterminisme Social* and *Le Problème du Déterminisme, Déterminisme Biologique et Déterminisme Social* by D. Draghiscesco', *Psychological Bulletin*, 2 (1905).

29 See May Jo Deegan (ed.), *George Herbert Mead. Essays in Social Psychology* (New Brunswick: Transaction Books, 2001).

30 Mead, *The Philosophy of the Act*, ed. Charles W. Morris et al. (Chicago: University of Chicago Press, 1938), p. 114.
31 Mead, *The Philosophy of the Present*, ed. Arthur E. Murphy (La Salle, IL: Open Court, 1932; Amherst, NY: Prometheus Books, repr. 2002), p. 173.

Chapter 3   Mead's Social Psychology: Basic Concepts

1 Mead, 'A Behavioristic Account of the Significant Symbol', *Journal of Philosophy*, 19 (1922), pp. 157–8.
2 As we shall see, Mead wishes to develop an integrated scientific explanation for two parallel developmental processes, namely the phylogenetic (human species) and ontogenetic (human individuals) evolution. The reconstruction of the way our self becomes the most important object in our world thus refers to the ontogenetic dimension of this endeavour.
3 Mead, *Mind, Self, and Society*, ed. Charles W. Morris (Chicago: University of Chicago Press, 1934; repr. 1997), p. 279.
4 Mead, *Mind, Self, and Society*, p. 136.
5 Mead, 'The Genesis of the Self and Social Control', *International Journal of Ethics*, 35 (1925), p. 272.
6 Mead, 'Genesis of the Self', p. 262.
7 Mead, 'The Social Self', *Journal of Philosophy, Psychology and Scientific Methods*, 10 (1913), p. 377.
8 Mead, *Mind, Self, and Society*, p. 244.
9 Mead, *Mind, Self, and Society*, p. 253.
10 Mead, 'Genesis of the Self', p. 267.
11 By 'gesture' Mead means an attitude or movement on the part of an organism, which is a stimulus for the response of 'other forms'. In other words, a gesture is but a phase of a larger social act.
12 Mead, *Mind, Self, and Society*, p. 236.
13 Mead, *Mind, Self, and Society*, p. 228.
14 'There exists thus a field of conduct even among animals below man, which in its nature may be classed as gesture. It consists of the beginnings of those actions which call out instinctive responses from other forms. And these beginnings of acts call out responses which lead to readjustments of acts which have been commenced, and these readjustments lead to still other beginnings of response which again call out still other readjustments. Thus there is a conversation of gesture . . .'. Mead, 'Social Consciousness and the Consciousness of Meaning', *Psychological Bulletin*, 7 (1910), p. 398.
15 Mead, *Mind, Self, and Society*, p. 81.
16 However, one would be wrong to assume that the 'unconscious conversation of gestures' is a mode of interaction which only occurred at the dawn of human evolution; on the contrary, it is a rather common type of social interaction, for it covers all activities involving unmindful readjustments such as boxing, one of Mead's favourite examples.
17 Mead, *Mind, Self, and Society*, p. 69.
18 Mead, *Mind, Self, and Society*, pp. 71–2.
19 Mead, 'Social Consciousness and the Consciousness of Meaning', p. 399.
20 Mead, *Mind, Self, and Society*, p. 89.

21 Mead, *Mind, Self, and Society*, p. 79.
22 Mead, *Mind, Self, and Society*, p. 80.
23 Mead, *Mind, Self, and Society*, p. 78.
24 Mead, *Mind, Self, and Society*, p. 267 n. 12.
25 Mead, *Mind, Self, and Society*, p. 268.
26 Even though, as Mead asserts on various occasions, the example of deaf-mutes alerts us to the possibility that the function of enabling humans to become objects to themselves is also performed by gestures other than the vocal ones. See e.g. Mead, 'Genesis of the Self', p. 271.
27 Mead, *Mind, Self, and Society*, p. 6 n6.
28 Mead, *Mind, Self, and Society*, p. 60.
29 Mead, 'The Social Self', p. 377.
30 I am thinking of Hans Joas, who claims that Mead's theory lacks a 'taxonomy of the various ways in which language can be pragmatically used'. *G. H. Mead. A Contemporary Re-examination of His Thought* (Cambridge, MA: MIT Press, 1985; repr. 1997), p. 117.
31 See Mead, *The Individual and the Social Self: Unpublished Work of George Herbert Mead*, ed. David L. Miller (Chicago: University of Chicago Press, 1982).
32 Mead, *The Individual and the Social Self*, p. 161.
33 Mead, 'A Behavioristic Account of the Significant Symbol', p. 161.
34 Mead, *Mind, Self, and Society*, p. 50.
35 Mead, *Mind, Self, and Society*, p. 133.
36 Mead, *Mind, Self, and Society*, p. 134.
37 Mead, *Mind, Self, and Society*, p. 191.

Chapter 4   The Social Self

1 Mead, *Mind, Self, and Society*, ed. Charles W. Morris (Chicago: University of Chicago Press, 1934; repr. 1997), p. 163.
2 Mead, *Mind, Self, and Society*, p. 91.
3 Mead, *Mind, Self, and Society*, p. 99.
4 Mead, *Mind, Self, and Society*, p. 100.
5 Mead, *Mind, Self, and Society*, p. 134.
6 Mead, *Mind, Self, and Society*, p. 186.
7 Mead, 'Consciousness, Mind, the Self, and Scientific Objects', in *The Individual and the Social Self: Unpublished Work of George Herbert Mead*, ed. David L. Miller (Chicago: University of Chicago Press, 1982), p. 177.
8 Mead, *Mind, Self, and Society*, p. 224 n26.
9 Mead, *Mind, Self, and Society*, p. 308.
10 Mead, *Mind, Self, and Society*, p. 144 n4.
11 Mead, *The Individual and the Social Self: Unpublished Work of George Herbert Mead*, ed. David L. Miller (Chicago: University of Chicago Press, 1982), pp. 163–4.
12 Mead, 'The Genesis of the Self and Social Control', *International Journal of Ethics*, 35 (1925), p. 269.
13 Mead, *Mind, Self, and Society*, p. 150.
14 Mead, 'The Genesis of the Self and Social Control', p. 269.

15 See Horace Thayer, *Meaning and Action, A Critical History of Pragmatism* (Indianapolis: Bobbs-Merrill Company, 1968), p. 57.

16 Mead, 'The Genesis of the Self and Social Control', p. 272.

17 Mead drew on William James on this topic. For James' conception of the dual structure of the self, see his *Principles of Psychology*, Vol. 1 (New York: Henry Holt, 1890).

18 Mead, *Mind, Self, and Society*, p. 216 n23.

19 Mead, *Mind, Self, and Society*, p. 214.

20 Mead, *Mind, Self, and Society*, p. 209.

21 Mead, *Mind, Self, and Society*, p. 218.

22 Mead, *Mind, Self, and Society*, p. 199.

23 Mead, 'Philanthropy from the point of view of ethics', in *Intelligent Philanthropy*, ed. E. Faris, F. Laune and A. J. Todd (Chicago: University of Chicago Press, 1930), p. 146.

24 Mead, *Mind, Self, and Society*, p. 196.

25 Mead, *Mind, Self, and Society*, p. 197.

Chapter 5   Society, Mind and Self

1 Mead, *Mind, Self, and Society*, ed. Charles W. Morris (Chicago: University of Chicago Press, 1934; repr. 1997), p. 273.

2 Mead, 'The Psychological Bases of Internationalism', *Survey*, 33 (1915), p. 604.

3 According to Joas, while Simmel conceives of war as a 'deeply moving existential experience of an ecstatic feeling of security that liberates our personality from old inhibitions', Durkheim, in his sociology of religion, describes 'collective effervescence' experiences as a 'group ecstasy that has the function of shaping identity and creating social bonds'. Hans Joas, *War and Modernity* (Cambridge: Polity Press, 2003), p. 65. Oddly, Joas fails to extend this parallel to Mead's thesis of the fusion between the 'I' and the 'me'.

4 Mead, 'The Psychology of Punitive Justice', *American Journal of Sociology*, 23 (1918), p. 598.

5 Mead, 'The Psychological Bases of Internationalism', p. 607.

6 Mead, 'The Psychological Bases of Internationalism', p. 605.

7 Mead, 'The Psychological Bases of Internationalism', p. 607.

8 Mead, 'National-Mindedness and International-Mindedness', *International Journal of Ethics*, 39 (1929), p. 393.

9 Mead, 'National-Mindedness and International-Mindedness', p. 395.

10 Mead, *Mind, Self, and Society*, p. 271.

11 Mead, 'National-Mindedness and International-Mindedness', pp. 403–4.

12 Mead, *Mind, Self, and Society*, p. 155.

13 Mead, *The Individual and the Social Self: Unpublished Work of George Herbert Mead*, ed. David L. Miller (Chicago: University of Chicago Press, 1982), p. 151.

14 On this issue, see Agnes Dodds, Jeanette Lawrence and Jaan Valsiner, 'The Personal and the Social. Mead's Theory of the "Generalized Other"', *Theory and Psychology*, 7 (1997).

15 Mead, *Mind, Self, and Society*, p. 254.
16 Mead, *Mind, Self, and Society*, p. 255.
17 Mead, *Mind, Self, and Society*, p. 201.
18 Skinner argues that historically minded inquiries into the past 'offer us an additional means of reflecting on what we believe, and thus of strengthening our present beliefs by way of testing them against alternative possibilities, or else of improving them if we come to recognize that the alternatives are both possible and desirable'. Quentin Skinner, 'A Reply to my Critics', in J. Tully (ed.), *Meaning and Context* (Cambridge: Polity Press, 1988), p. 287.
19 Mead, 'The Genesis of the Self and Social Control', *International Journal of Ethics*, 35 (1925), p. 276.
20 Mead, *Mind, Self, and Society*, p. 229.
21 Mead, *Mind, Self, and Society*, p. 262.
22 Mead, *Mind, Self, and Society*, p. 386.
23 Mead, *Mind, Self, and Society*, p. 202.
24 Mead, 'Scientific Method and the Moral Sciences', *International Journal of Ethics*, 33 (1923), p. 237.
25 Mead, 'Scientific Method and the Moral Sciences', p. 244.
26 In a book published shortly after Mead's article, *The Public and Its Problems* (1927), Dewey subscribes to a similar position to the one argued by Mead. Dewey writes: 'Majority rule, just as majority rule, is as foolish as its critics charge it with being. But it never is *merely* majority rule. . . . The essential need, in other words, is the improvement of the methods and conditions of debate, discussion and persuasion. That is *the* problem of the public'. John Dewey, *The Public and Its Problems*, in *The Later Works, 1925–1927*, Vol. 2 (Carbondale: Southern Illinois University Press, 1984), p. 365. This pragmatist understanding of democratic politics is of central importance for Habermas's discursive conception of deliberative democracy. Habermas acknowledges this fact in his latest major political work, where he quotes Dewey's words approvingly. See Jürgen Habermas, *Between Facts and Norms. Contributions to a Discourse Theory of Law and Democracy* (Cambridge: Polity Press, 1996), p. 304.
27 Mead, *Mind, Self, and Society*, p. 178.
28 Mead, *The Philosophy of the Act*, ed. Charles Morris et al. (Chicago: University of Chicago Press, 1938), p. 364.
29 It is important to note that, while discussing the stage of manipulation, Mead points out the distinction between 'perceptual objects', understood as means for the consummation of the act (e.g. an apple is grabbed by an individual who then eats it), which include past events, and 'scientific objects', conceived of as entities of thought. See *The Philosophy of the Act*, pp. 16–22.
30 Mead, *Mind, Self, and Society*, p. 363.
31 Mead explains: 'The social process, then, does not depend for its origin or initial existence upon the existence and interaction of selves; though it does depend upon the latter for the higher stages of complexity and organization which it reaches after selves have arisen within it.' Mead, *Mind, Self, and Society*, p. 226.
32 Mead, *Mind, Self, and Society*, p. 138.

33 Mead exemplifies the social relation to nature and its objects in the following manner: 'It is perhaps most evident in the irritations against total depravity of inanimate things, in our affection for familiar objects of constant employment, and in the aesthetic attitude toward nature which is the source of all nature poetry.' *Mind, Self, and Society*, p. 378.

34 Mead, *Mind, Self, and Society*, p. 184.

35 Mead, *Mind, Self, and Society*, p. 249.

36 Mead, *Mind, Self, and Society*, p. 379.

37 See Mead, *The Philosophy of the Act*, pp. 445–53.

38 Despite the analytical distinction between the various stages of the act, and in contrast to a mechanistic perspective, Mead emphasizes the unity of the act. Referring to the act of eating, Mead says: 'Want, interest, and satisfaction – each implies the entire process and embodies it in a particular phase. In this respect they are not composite parts of the act, though the different stages are parts of the whole as a process. In experience, as in life as an entity, the whole is given in the part. In contrast with this, in a mechanism the whole arises out of its parts.' Mead, *The Philosophy of the Act*, p. 452.

Chapter 6 Mead and Symbolic Interactionism

1 Filipe Carreira da Silva, 'G. H. Mead in the History of Sociological Ideas', *Journal of the History of Behavioral Sciences*, 42 (2006).

2 On the Parsons–Mead relationship, see Herbert Blumer, Talcott Parsons and Jonathan Turner, 'Exchange on Turner, "Parsons as a Symbolic Interactionist"', *Sociological Inquiry*, 45 (1975).

3 Dmitri Shalin, 'Pragmatism and Social Interactionism', *American Sociological Review*, 51 (1986).

4 Arguably the best work on the 'Chicago school' is David Bulmer, *The Chicago School of Sociology: Institutionalization, Diversity, and the Rise of Sociology* (Chicago: University of Chicago Press, 1984). Also noteworthy are Berenice Fisher and Anselm Strauss, 'Interactionism', in T. Bottomore and R. Nisbet (eds), *A History of Sociological Analysis* (New York: Oxford University Press, 1978) and Robert E. Faris, *Chicago Sociology 1920–32* (Chicago: University of Chicago Press, 1967).

5 See H. Joas, 'Symbolic Interactionism', in Anthony Giddens and Jonathan Turner (eds), *Social Theory Today* (Cambridge: Polity Press, 1987).

6 See Roscoe Hinkle, *Founding Theory of American Sociology 1881–1915* (London: Routledge & Kegan Paul, 1980), pp. 24–9.

7 On this matter, see J. David Lewis and Robert Smith, *American Sociology and Pragmatism: Mead, Chicago Sociology, and Symbolic Interaction* (Chicago: University of Chicago Press, 1980).

8 H. Joas, *Pragmatism and Social Theory* (Chicago: University of Chicago Press, 1993), p. 90.

9 Robert E. Faris, *Chicago Sociology, 1920–32* (San Francisco: Chandler Publishing Company, 1967).

10 Lewis and Smith, *American Sociology and Pragmatism*, p. 233.

11 Blumer quoted in Lewis and Smith, *American Sociology and Pragmatism*, p. 239.

12 Herbert Blumer, *George Herbert Mead and Human Conduct*, ed. Thomas J. Morrione (Walnut Creek, CA: Altamira Press, 2004), p. 3.
13 For an analysis of Blumer's relation with the American philosophical tradition, see Charles Tucker, 'Herbert Blumer: A Pilgrimage with Pragmatism', *Symbolic Interaction*, 11 (1988).
14 Blumer, *George Herbert Mead and Human Conduct*, p. 180.
15 Herbert Blumer, 'Comment on Lewis' "The Classic American Pragmatists as Forerunners to Symbolic Interactionism"', *Sociological Quarterly*, 18 (1977), p. 286.
16 Blumer quoted in Lewis and Smith, *American Sociology and Pragmatism*, p. 170.
17 Herbert Blumer, 'An Appraisal of Thomas and Znaniecki's "The Polish Peasant in Europe and America"', in *Critiques of Research in the Social Sciences* (New York: Transaction, 1939).
18 Herbert Blumer, 'Social Psychology', in *Man and Society. A Substantial Introduction to the Social Sciences*, ed. Emerson Schmidt (New York: Prentice-Hall, 1937).
19 Blumer, *George Herbert Mead and Human Conduct*, p. 31.
20 Blumer, *Symbolic Interactionism. Perspective and Method* (Berkeley: University of California Press, 1969), p. 2.
21 Blumer, *Symbolic Interactionism*, p. 7.
22 Blumer, *Symbolic Interactionism*, p. 12.
23 Herbert Blumer, *Industrialization as an Agent of Social Change: A Critical Analysis*, ed. D. Maines and T. Morrione (New York: Aldine de Gruyter, 1990).
24 Blumer, *Symbolic Interactionism*, p. 62.
25 Blumer, *Symbolic Interactionism*, p. 63.
26 Blumer, *Symbolic Interactionism*, p. 64.
27 Blumer, *Symbolic Interactionism*, p. 66.
28 Mead, *Mind, Self, and Society*, p. 77.
29 Blumer, *Symbolic Interactionism*, p. 14.
30 Mead, *Mind, Self, and Society*, p. 78.
31 Blumer, *Symbolic Interactionism*, pp. 73–4.
32 Herbert Blumer, 'George Herbert Mead', in Buford Rhea (ed.), *The Future of Sociological Classics* (London: George Allen and Unwin, 1981), p. 161.
33 On this subject, see my 'Re-examining Mead: G. H. Mead on the "Material Reproduction of Society"', *Journal of Classical Sociology*, 7 (2007).
34 See Manford Kuhn and Thomas S. McPartland, 'An Empirical Investigation of Self-Attitudes', *American Sociological Review*, 19 (1954). An online copy of the TST is available at: http://www.hum.utah.edu/communication/classes/fa02/1010-5/twentystatements.pdf (last accessed 2 March 2007).
35 Manford Kuhn, 'Major Trends in Symbolic Interaction Theory in the Past Twenty-Five Years', *The Sociological Quarterly*, 5 (1964).
36 Kuhn, 'Major Trends', p. 64.
37 Kuhn, 'Major Trends', p. 79.
38 E.g. Carl J. Couch, 'Symbolic Interaction and Generic Sociological Principles', *Symbolic Interaction*, 8 (1984); Carl J. Couch, *Researching Social Processes in the Laboratory* (Greenwich: JAI Press, 1987).

39 Anselm Strauss, *Negotiations: Varieties, Contexts, Processes, and Social Order* (San Francisco: Jossey-Bass Publishers, 1978), p. 18.
40 Strauss, *Negotiations*, p. 235.
41 Strauss, *Negotiations*, pp. 237–8.
42 David R. Maines, 'Social Organization and Social Structure in Symbolic Interactionist Thought', *Annual Review of Sociology*, 3 (1977), p. 244.
43 Howard S. Becker, *Outsiders. Studies in Sociology of Deviance* (New York: The Free Press, 1963), p. 182.
44 Becker, *Outsiders*, p. 189.
45 Becker, *Outsiders*, p. 20.
46 Becker, *Outsiders*, p. 9.
47 Becker, *Outsiders*, p. 188.
48 Erving Goffman, *The Presentation of the Self in Everyday Life* (New York: Anchor Books, 1959), p. 22.
49 Goffman, *The Presentation of the Self*, p. 56.
50 Goffman, *The Presentation of the Self*, pp. 252–3.
51 Mead, *Mind, Self, and Society*, p. 161.
52 Gary Alan Fine, 'The Sad Demise, Mysterious Disappearance, and Glorious Triumph of Symbolic Interactionism', *Annual Review of Sociology*, 19 (1993), p. 71.
53 Mead, 'The Philosophy of John Dewey', *International Journal of Ethics*, 46 (1935–6), p. 70.

Chapter 7 Mead and Twentieth-Century Sociology

1 Emile Durkheim, *Pragmatisme et Sociologie* (Paris: Vrin, 1955). On Durkheim's critical reception of pragmatism, see Hans Joas, 'Durkheim et le pragmatisme. La Psychologie de la conscience et la constitution sociale des catégories', *Revue Française de Sociologie*, 25 (1984).
2 Scheler quoted in Karl-Siegbert Rehberg, 'Arnold Gehlen's Elementary Anthropology – An Introduction', in *Man: His Nature and Place in the World* (New York: Columbia University Press, 1988), p. xiv.
3 Axel Honneth and Hans Joas, *Social Action and Human Nature* (Cambridge: Cambridge University Press, 1988), p. 51.
4 Gehlen quoted in Honneth and Joas, *Social Action*, p. 51.
5 Arnold Gehlen, *Man: His Nature and Place in the World* (New York: Columbia University Press, 1988), p. 5.
6 Gehlen, *Man*, p. 13.
7 See chapter 2, note 20.
8 Gehlen quoted in Honneth and Joas, *Social Action*, p. 59.
9 Gehlen, *Man*, p. 196.
10 Gehlen, *Man*, p. 195.
11 Gehlen, *Man*, pp. 254–5.
12 Gehlen, *Man*, p. 195.
13 Louis Menand, *The Metaphysical Club: A Story of Ideas in America* (New York: Farrar, Straus, and Giroux, 2001).
14 Jürgen Habermas, 'A Philosophico-Political Profile', *New Left Review*, 151 (1985), pp. 76–7.

15 Gisela Hinkle, 'Habermas, Mead, and Rationality', *Symbolic Interaction*, 15 (1992), p. 320.
16 Max Horkheimer, 'Traditional and Critical Theory', in Paul Connerton (ed.), *Critical Sociology* (New York: Penguin, 1976), p. 223.
17 Theodor Adorno, *Critique of Pure Tolerance* (Boston: Beacon Press, 1965), p. 105.
18 See Jürgen Habermas, 'Postscript. Some Concluding Remarks', in M. Mitchell Aboulafia, Myra Brookman and Catherine Kemp (eds), *Habermas and Pragmatism* (London: Routledge, 2002), p. 227.
19 Gehlen quoted in Jürgen Habermas, *Postmetaphysical Thinking: Philosophical Essays* (Cambridge: Polity Press, 1988), p. 149.
20 Habermas, *Postmetaphysical Thinking*, pp. 152–3.
21 Habermas, *Postmetaphysical Thinking*, p. 177.
22 Habermas, *Postmetaphysical Thinking*, p. 187.
23 Habermas, *Postmetaphysical Thinking*, p. 187.
24 Habermas, *Postmetaphysical Thinking*, p. 188.
25 Habermas, *Postmetaphysical Thinking*, p. 187.
26 Habermas, *Postmetaphysical Thinking*, p. 182.
27 Jürgen Habermas, *The Theory of Communicative Action. Volume 2. Lifeworld and System: A Critique of Functionalist Reason* (Cambridge: Polity Press, 1985), p. 16.
28 Habermas, *The Theory of Communicative Action. Volume 2*, p. 27.
29 See Habermas, *The Theory of Communicative Action. Volume 2*, pp. 29–42.
30 Habermas, *The Theory of Communicative Action. Volume 2*, p. 44.
31 Habermas, *The Theory of Communicative Action. Volume 2*, p. 107. The rationalization of the lifeworld comprehends two interrelated processes: firstly, the gradual differentiation of the structural components of the lifeworld (culture, society and person); secondly, there are changes within each of these components: sacred knowledge gives way to rational scientific knowledge; law and morals become separated and are universalized; individualism constitutes an increasingly common feature of modern industrial societies.
32 Habermas, *The Theory of Communicative Action. Volume 2*, p. 110.
33 Anthony Giddens' structuration theory (as presented in *The Constitution of Society*, 1984) and Pierre Bourdieu's theory of practice (e.g. *La Distinction*, 1979) are the two most obvious examples.
34 Hans Joas, *Pragmatism and Social Theory* (Chicago: University of Chicago Press, 1993), p. 239.
35 H. Joas, *G. H. Mead. A Contemporary Re-examination of His Thought* (Cambridge, MA: MIT Press, 1985; repr. 1985), pp. 145–98.
36 Gary A. Cook and Dmitri Shalin raise this particular objection. See Joas, *Pragmatism and Social Theory*, p. 242.
37 Cook, *George Herbert Mead. The Making of a Social Pragmatist* (Urbana, IL: University of Illinois Press, 1993).
38 See Filipe Carreira da Silva, *In Dialogue with Modern Times. The Social and Political Thought of G. H. Mead* (Lanham, MD: Lexington Books, forthcoming).
39 Joas, *G. H. Mead*, p. 19.
40 Joas, *G. H. Mead*, p. 23.

41 I have in mind Dmitri Shalin. See, for example, his 'G. H. Mead, Socialism, and the Progressive Agenda', *American Journal of Sociology*, 93 (1988).

42 Axel Honneth, *The Fragmented World of the Social. Essays in Social and Political Philosophy* (New York: SUNY Press, 1995), p. xxiii.

43 Honneth, *The Fragmented World of the Social*, p. xiv.

44 Axel Honneth, *Struggles for Recognition. The Moral Grammar of Social Conflicts* (Cambridge, MA: MIT Press, 1996), p. 71.

45 Honneth, *The Fragmented World of the Social*, p. xxiii.

46 Honneth, *Struggles for Recognition*, p. 75.

47 Honneth, *Struggles for Recognition*, p. 78.

48 Honneth, *Struggles for Recognition*, p. 80.

49 Ibid.

50 Mead quoted in Honneth, *Struggles for Recognition*, p. 81 n20.

51 Honneth, *Struggles for Recognition*, p. 84.

52 Honneth, *Struggles for Recognition*, p. 88.

53 Honneth, *Struggles for Recognition*, p. 89.

54 Honneth, *Struggles for Recognition*, p. 91.

55 Honneth, *The Fragmented World of the Social*, p. xxiv.

56 Honneth, *The Fragmented World of the Social*, p. 267.

57 Patchen Markell, 'The Potential and the Actual: Mead, Honneth, and the 'I''', in Bert van den Brink and David Owen (eds), *Recognition and Power* (Cambridge: Cambridge University Press, 2006).

58 Mead, *Mind, Self, and Society*, ed. Charles W. Morris (Chicago: University of Chicago Press, 1934; repr. 1997), p. 204.

59 Markell, 'The Potential and the Actual', p. 8, online version: http://www.polisci.umn.edu/kiosk/link tunnel.php?id=9326&user= (last accessed 2 March 2007).

60 Randall Collins, 'Toward a Neo-Meadian Sociology of Mind', in P. Hamilton (ed.), *George Herbert Mead: Critical Assessments*, 4 vols (London: Routledge, 1992), IV, p. 263.

61 I am referring to Randall Collins, *Conflict Sociology: Toward an Explanatory Science* (New York: Academic Press, 1975).

62 Randall Collins, 'Functional and Conflict Theories of Educational Stratification', *American Sociological Review*, 36 (1971), p. 1009.

63 Collins, *Conflict Sociology*, pp. 79–87.

64 Randall Collins, *The Credential Society: An Historical Sociology of Education and Stratification* (New York: Academic Press, 1979).

65 Collins, *The Credential Society*, p. 48.

66 Collins, 'Toward a Neo-Meadian Sociology of Mind', p. 291.

67 Collins, 'Toward a Neo-Meadian Sociology of Mind', p. 281. See also Randall Collins, 'On the Micro-Foundations of Macro-sociology', *American Journal of Sociology*, 86 (1981).

68 Collins, 'Toward a Neo-Meadian Sociology of Mind', p. 275.

69 Collins, 'Toward a Neo-Meadian Sociology of Mind', p. 277.

70 Randall Collins, *Interaction Ritual Chains* (Princeton, NJ: Princeton University Press, 2004), p. 4.

71 Collins, *Interaction Ritual Chains*, p. 48.

72 Collins, *Interaction Ritual Chains*, pp. 76–7.

73 Collins, *Interaction Ritual Chains*, p. 373.

74 Collins, *Interaction Ritual Chains*, p. 205.
75 Jeffrey C. Alexander, *Twenty Lectures: Sociological Theory after 1945* (New York: Columbia University Press, 1987).
76 Alexander, *Twenty Lectures*, p. 214.
77 Jeffrey C. Alexander, *Neofunctionalism and After* (Oxford: Blackwell, 1998), p. 11.
78 Alexander, *Neofunctionalism and After*, p. 215.
79 Alexander, *Neofunctionalism and After*, p. 214.
80 Alexander, *Neofunctionalism and After*, p. 216.
81 Ibid.
82 Alexander, *Neofunctionalism and After*, p. 220.
83 Alexander, *Neofunctionalism and After*, p. 217.
84 Alexander, *Neofunctionalism and After*, p. 57.
85 Alexander, *Neofunctionalism and After*, p. 73.
86 Alexander, *Neofunctionalism and After*, p. 222.
87 Alexander, *Neofunctionalism and After*, p. 227.
88 Alexander, *Neofunctionalism and After*, p. 228.
89 E.g. Jeffrey C. Alexander, 'Cultural Pragmatics: Social Performance Between Ritual and Strategy', *Sociological Theory*, 22 (2004).

Chapter 8   Why Read Mead Today?

1 Alberto Melucci, *The Playing Self. Person and Meaning in the Planetary Society* (Cambridge: Cambridge University Press, 1996), p. 47.
2 See Charles Hartshorne, *Creativity in American Philosophy* (Albany, NY: SUNY Press, 1984).
3 See, for instance, the excellent study by Douglas Anderson, *Creativity and the Philosophy of C. S. Peirce* (Dordrecht: M. Nijhoff, 1987).
4 See Hans Joas, 'The Democratization of Differentiation: On the Creativity of Collective Action', in Jeffrey C. Alexander and Piotr Stompka (eds), *Rethinking Progress* (Boston: Unwin, 1990); *The Creativity of Action* (Cambridge: Polity Press, 1996); José Maurício Domingues, *Social Creativity, Collective Subjectivity and Contemporary Modernity* (Basingstoke: Macmillan Press, 2000); Anthony Giddens, *The Consequences of Modernity* (Cambridge: Polity Press, 1990); Michael Mann, *The Sources of Social Power, Vol. 2. The Rise of Classes and Nation-States, 1760–1914* (Cambridge: Cambridge University Press, 1993); Craig Calhoun, *Critical Social Theory* (Oxford: Blackwell, 1995).
5 Peter Wagner, *A Sociology of Modernity. Liberty and Discipline* (London: Routledge, 1994).
6 Karl Mannheim, *Ideology and Utopia: An Introduction to the Sociology of Knowledge* (London: Routledge, 1972), p. 222.
7 See Talcott Parsons, *The Structure of Social Action, Vols I–II* (New York: Free Press, 1937; repr. 1968); Herbert Marcuse, *Reason and Revolution: Hegel and the Rise of Social Theory* (London: Routledge, 1941; repr. 1973).
8 T. H. Marshall, *Class, Citizenship, and Social Development* (Garden City, NY: Doubleday, 1964).

9 Talcott Parsons, *The Social System* (Glencoe, IL: Free Press, 1951), p. 25.

10 Jean-François Lyotard, *La Condition Postmoderne* (Paris: Minuit, 1979). See also Ulrich Beck, Anthony Giddens and Scott Lash, *Reflexive Modernization: Politics, Tradition and Aesthetics in the Modern Social Order* (Cambridge: Polity Press, 1994).

11 Zygmunt Bauman, *Modernity and Ambivalence* (Cambridge: Polity Press, 1991), p. 272.

12 Shmuel N. Eisenstadt, 'Multiple Modernities', in S. N. Eisenstadt (ed.), *Multiple Modernities* (London: Transaction Publishers, 2002); Göran Therborn, 'Entangled Modernities', *European Journal of Social Theory*, 6 (2003).

13 Eisenstadt, 'Multiple Modernities', p. 23.

14 Eisenstadt, 'Multiple Modernities', p. 14.

15 Therborn, 'Entangled Modernities', p. 295

16 Melucci, *The Playing Self*, p. 43.

17 Michel Maffesoli, *Le Temps des tribus. Le déclin de l'individualisme dans les sociétés de masse* (Paris: Méridiens Klincksieck, 1988).

18 Zygmunt Bauman, *Liquid Modernity* (Cambridge: Polity Press, 2000), p. 85.

19 For an exploration of this insight by a political theorist see Russell Hardin, *Indeterminacy and Society* (Princeton, NJ: Princeton University Press, 2003).

20 Mead, *Mind, Self, and Society*, ed. Charles W. Morris (Chicago: University of Chicago Press, 1934; repr. 1997), p. 221.

21 See Agnes Dodds, Jeanette Lawrence and Jaan Valsiner, 'The Personal and the Social. Mead's Theory of the "Generalized Other"', *Theory and Psychology*, 7 (1997); Alex Gillespie, 'G. H. Mead: Theorist of the Social Act', *Journal for the Theory of Social Behaviour*, 35 (2005).

22 E.g. Robert Perinbanayagam, *Signifying Acts: Structure and Meaning in Everyday Life* (Carbondale, IL: Southern Illinois University Press, 1985).

23 http://spartan.ac.brocku.ca/~lward/Mead/default.html (last accessed 2 March 2007).

24 Lewis Coser, 'George Herbert Mead', in *Masters of Sociological Thought: Ideas in Historical and Social Context* (New York: Harcourt Brace Jovanovich, 1971), pp. 333–55.

25 David L. Miller, *George Herbert Mead. Self, Language and the World* (Chicago: University of Chicago Press, 1973), p. ix.

26 H. Joas, *G. H. Mead. A Contemporary Re-examination of His Thought* (Cambridge, MA: MIT Press, 1985; repr. 1997), p. 1.

27 Andrew Feffer, *The Chicago Pragmatists and American Progressivism* (Ithaca: Cornell University Press, 1993), pp. 2, 10–11.

28 G. A. Cook, *George Herbert Mead. The Making of a Social Pragmatist* (Urbana, IL: University of Illinois Press, 1993), p. xiv.

29 See Coser, 'George Herbert Mead', pp. 345–6.

30 Miller, *George Herbert Mead*, p. 24.

31 See Miller, *George Herbert Mead*, p. 188.

32 I am referring to Joas' aforementioned *G. H. Mead. A Contemporary Re-examination of His Thought*.

33 As Joas acknowledges in his introduction, Mead's discussion of physics, history of philosophy and educational theory were not given systematic attention. See Joas, *G. H. Mead*, pp. 12–13.

34 This is precisely what my doctoral dissertation aimed to provide – a discussion of the several pillars of Mead's system of thought in the light of their evolution from the early 1890s until 1931. Carreira da Silva, *In Dialogue with Modern Times. The Social and Political Thought of G. H. Mead* (Lanham, MD: Lexington Books, forthcoming).

Bibliography

Primary

A chronological listing of George Herbert Mead's published works

1881: 'The Relation of Art to Morality', *Oberlin Review*, 9: 63–4.

1882: 'Charles Lamb', *Oberlin Review*, 10: 15–6.

1882: 'De Quincey', *Oberlin Review*, 10: 50–2.

1883: 'John Locke', *Oberlin Review*, 10: 217–19.

1884: 'Republican Persecution', *The Nation*, 39: 519–20.

1894: 'The Problem of Psychological Measurement', in *Proceedings of the American Psychological Association* (New York: Macmillan), pp. 22–3.

1894: 'The Greek Mysteries', *University of Michigan Record*, 1: 102.

1894: 'Herr Lasswitz on Energy and Epistemology', *Psychological Review*, 1: 172–5.

1894: 'Review of *Die Moderne Energetik in ihrer Bedeutung für die Erkenntniskritik* by K. Lasswitz', *Psychological Review*, 1: 210–13.

1895: 'Review of *An Introduction to Comparative Psychology* by C. Lloyd Morgan', *Psychological Review*, 2: 399–402.

1895: 'A Theory of Emotions from the Physiological Standpoint', *Psychological Review*, 2: 162–4.

1896: 'Some Aspects of Greek Philosophy', *University of Chicago Record*, 1: 42.

1896: 'The Relation of Play to Education', *University of Chicago Record*, 1: 141–5.

1897: 'Review of *Untersuchungen zur Phänomenologie und Ontologie des Menschlichen Geistes* by Gustav Class', *American Journal of Theology*, 1: 789–92.

1898: 'The Child and His Environment', *Transactions of the Illinois Society for Child-Study*, 3: 1–11.

1899: 'The Working Hypothesis in Social Reform', *American Journal of Sociology*, 5: 367–71.

1899: 'Review of *The Psychology of Socialism* by Gustave Le Bon', *American Journal of Sociology*, 5: 404–12.

1900: 'Suggestions Towards a Theory of the Philosophical Disciplines', *Philosophical Review*, 9: 1–17.

1900–1: 'Review of *Philosophie des Geldes* by Georg Simmel', *Journal of Political Economy*, 9: 616–19.

1901: 'A New Criticism of Hegelianism: Is It Valid? A Review of *Idealism and Theology: A Study of Presuppositions* by Charles F. D'Arcy', *American Journal of Theology*, 5: 87–96.

1903: 'The Definition of the Psychical', in *Decennial Publications of the University of Chicago*, First Series, 3 (Chicago: University of Chicago Press), pp. 77–112.

1904: 'The Basis for a Parents' Association', *Elementary School Teacher*, 4: 337–46.

1904: 'Image or Sensation', *Journal of Philosophy, Psychology and Scientific Method*, 1: 604–7.

1904: 'The Relations of Psychology and Philology', *Psychological Bulletin*, 1: 375–91.

1905: 'Review of *Du Rôle de l'individu dans le déterminisme social* and *Le Problème du déterminisme, déterminisme biologique et déterminisme social* by D. Draghicesco', *Psychological Bulletin*, 2: 399–405.

1905: 'Review of *Etudes sur la sélection chez l'homme* by Paul Jacoby', *Psychological Bulletin*, 2: 407–12.

1906: 'Science in the High School', *School Review*, 14: 237–49.

1906: 'The Imagination in Wundt's Treatment of Myth and Religion', *Psychological Bulletin*, 3: 393–9.

1906: 'The Teaching of Science in College', *Science*, 24: 390–7.

1907: 'Concerning Animal Perception', *Psychological Review*, 14: 383–90.

1907: 'Editorial Notes: School System in Chicago', *School Review*, 15: 160–5.

1907: 'Review of *The Newer Ideals of Peace* by Jane Addams', *American Journal of Sociology*, 13: 121–8.

1907: 'Review of *L'Evolution créatrice* by Henri Bergson', *Psychological Bulletin*, 4: 379–84.

1907: 'The Relation of Imitation to the Theory of Animal Perception', *Psychological Bulletin*, 4: 210–11.

1907–8: 'The Educational Situation in the Chicago Public Schools', *City Club Bulletin*, 1: 131–8.

1907–8: 'The Social Settlement, Its Basis and Function', *University of Chicago Record*, 12: 108–10.

1907–8: 'Editorial Notes: Policy Statement of the *Elementary School Teacher*', *Elementary School Teacher*, 8: 281–4.

1907–8: 'Editorial Notes: Industrial Education and Trade Schools', *Elementary School Teacher*, 8: 402–6.

1908: 'Educational Aspects of Trade Schools', *Union Labor Advocate*, 8: 19–20.

1908: 'The Philosophical Basis of Ethics', *International Journal of Ethics*, 18: 311–23.

1908: 'Review of *An Introduction to Social Psychology* by William McDougall', *Psychological Bulletin*, 5: 385–91.

1908: 'Review of *L'Idéal moderne* by Paul Gaultier', *Psychological Bulletin*, 5: 403–4.

1908–9: 'Editorial Notes: Resolution on Industrial Training', *Elementary School Teacher*, 9: 156–7.

1908–9: 'Editorial Notes: Industrial Training', *Elementary School Teacher*, 9: 212–14.

1908–9: 'Editorial Notes: Moral Training in the Schools', *Elementary School Teacher*, 9: 327–8.

1908–9: 'Industrial Education, the Working-Man, and the School', *Elementary School Teacher*, 9: 369–83.

1908–9: 'Editorial Notes: The Problem of History in Elementary School', *Elementary School Teacher*, 9: 433–4.

1909: 'Social Psychology as Counterpart to Physiological Psychology', *Psychological Bulletin*, 6: 401–8.

1909: 'The Adjustment of Our Industry to Surplus and Unskilled Labor', *Proceedings of the National Conference of Charities and Corrections*, 34: 222–5.

1910: 'Social Consciousness and the Consciousness of Meaning', *Psychological Bulletin*, 7: 397–405.

1910: 'The Psychology of Social Consciousness Implied in Instruction', *Science*, 31: 688–93.

1910: 'What Social Objects Does Psychology Presuppose?', *Psychological Bulletin*, 7: 52–3.

1910: 'What Social Objects Must Psychology Presuppose?', *Journal of Philosophy, Psychology and Scientific Methods*, 7: 174–80.

1911: 'Review of *Individualism: Four Lectures on the Significance of Consciousness for Social Relations* by Warner Fite', *Psychological Bulletin*, 8: 323–8.

1911: 'Review of *Social Value. A Study in Economic Theory* by B. M. Anderson, Jr.', *Psychological Bulletin*, 8: 432–6.

1912: 'The Mechanism of Social Consciousness', *Journal of Philosophy, Psychology and Scientific Methods*, 9: 401–6.

1912: co-author with Ernest A. Wreidt and William J. Bogan, *A Report on Vocational Training in Chicago and in other Cities* (Chicago: University of Chicago Press).

1912: 'A Report of the Public Education Committee of the City Club of Chicago', *City Club Bulletin*, 5: 373–83.

1912: 'Exhibit of the City Club Committee on Public Education', *City Club Bulletin*, 5: 9.

1912: 'Probation and Politics', *Survey*, 27: 2004–14. 1912: 'Remarks on Labor Night Concerning Participation of Representatives of Labor in the City Club', *City Club Bulletin*, 5: 214–15.

1913: 'The Social Self', *Journal of Philosophy, Psychology and Scientific Methods*, 10: 374–80.

1914: 'A Heckling School Board and an Educational Stateswoman', *Survey*, 31: 443–4.

1915: 'Natural Rights and the Theory of the Political Institution', *Journal of Philosophy*, 12: 141–55.

1915: 'Constitutional and Political Guarantees', *Philosophical Review*, 24: 193–4.

1915: 'The Psychological Bases of Internationalism', *Survey*, 33: 604–7.

1915: 'The Larger Educational Bearings of Vocational Guidance', in Meyer Bloomfield (ed.), *Readings in Vocational Guidance* (Boston: Ginn), pp. 43–55.

1915: 'Madison', *Survey*, 35: 349–51, 354–61.

1915: 'A Rejoinder', *Survey*, 35: 607, 610.

1916–17: 'Professor Hoxie and the Community', *University of Chicago Magazine*, 9: 114–17.

1917: 'The Conscientious Objector', *National Security League, Patriotism through Education Series*, 33: 1–10.

1917: 'Germany's Crisis – Its Effect on Labor, Part I', *Chicago Herald*, 26 July.

1917: 'Germany's Crisis – Its Effect on Labor, Part II', *Chicago Herald*, 27 July.

1917: 'War Issues to US Forced by Kaiser', *Chicago Herald*, 2 August.

1917: 'America's Ideals and the War', *Chicago Herald*, 3 August.

1917: 'Democracy's Issues in the World War', *Chicago Herald*, 4 August.

1917: 'Josiah Royce – A Personal Impression', *International Journal of Ethics*, 27: 168–70.

1917: 'Scientific Method and Individual Thinker', in John Dewey et al. (eds), *Creative Intelligence: Essays in the Pragmatic Attitude* (New York: Henry Holt), pp. 176–227.

1917: 'Review of *Truancy and Non-Attendance in the Chicago Schools* by Edith Abbott and Sophonisba P. Breckinridge', *Survey*, 38: 369–70.

1918: 'The Psychology of Punitive Justice', *American Journal of Sociology*, 23: 577–602.

1918: 'Review of *The Nature of Peace and the Terms of Its Perpetuation* by Thorstein Veblen', *Journal of Political Economy*, 26: 752–62.

1918: 'Social Work, Standards of Living and the War', *Proceedings of the National Conference of Social Work*, 45: 637–44.

1919: 'Mead Answers McCormick as to the League of Nations', *Chicago Evening Post*, 7 March.

1919: 'The League and the Community', *Bulletin of the Vocational Supervision League*, 1 (15 April).

1919: 'A Translation of *Folk Psychology* by Wilhelm Wundt', *American Journal of Theology*, 23: 533–6.

1920: 'Retiring President's Address', *City Club Bulletin*, 13: 94–5.

1921: 'Idea', in Shailer Mathews and Gerald Birney Smith (eds), *A Dictionary of Religion and Ethics* (New York: Macmillan), 215–16.

1921: 'Ideal', in Shailer Mathews and Gerald Birney Smith (eds), *A Dictionary of Religion and Ethics* (New York: Macmillan), p. 216.

1921: 'Individualism', in Shailer Mathews and Gerald Birney Smith (eds), *A Dictionary of Religion and Ethics* (New York: Macmillan), p. 222.

1921: 'Infinity', in Shailer Mathews and Gerald Birney Smith (eds), *A Dictionary of Religion and Ethics* (New York: Macmillan), p. 223.

1921: 'Law of Nature, Natural Law', in Shailer Mathews and Gerald Birney Smith (eds), *A Dictionary of Religion and Ethics* (New York: Macmillan), pp. 254–5.

1922: 'A Behavioristic Account of the Significant Symbol', *Journal of Philosophy*, 19: 157–63.

1923: 'Scientific Method and the Moral Sciences', *International Journal of Ethics*, 33: 229–47.

1924: 'Review of *The Domain of Natural Science* by E. W. Hobson', *Journal of Religion*, 4: 324–7.

1924: 'Ella Adams Moore', *Bulletin of the Vocational Supervision League*.

1925: 'The Genesis of the Self and Social Control', *International Journal of Ethics*, 35: 251–77.

1926: 'The Nature of Aesthetic Experience', *International Journal of Ethics*, 36: 382–92; afterwards published in *Selected Writings. George Herbert Mead*, ed. Andrew Reck (Chicago: University of Chicago Press, 1964; repr. 1981), pp. 294–305.

1926: 'The Objective Reality of Perspectives', in Edgar S. Brightman (ed.), *Proceedings of the Sixth International Congress of Philosophy* (New York: Longmans and Green), pp. 75–85; repr. in George Herbert Mead, *Philosophy of the Present*, ed. Arthur E. Murphy (La Salle, IL: Open Court, 1932; Amherst, NY: Prometheus Books, repr. 2002), pp. 171–82.

1929: 'A Pragmatic Theory of Truth', *University of California Publications in Philosophy*, 11: 65–88.

1929: 'Bishop Berkeley and his Message', *Journal of Philosophy*, 26: 421–30.

1929: 'National-Mindedness and International-Mindedness', *International Journal of Ethics*, 39: 385–407.

1929: 'The Nature of the Past', in John Coss (ed.), *Essays in Honor of John Dewey* (New York: Henry Holt), pp. 235–42.

1930: 'Cooley's Contribution to American Social Thought', *American Journal of Sociology*, 35: 693–706.

1930: 'Philanthropy from the Point of View of Ethics', in Ellsworth Faris, Ferris Laune and Arthur J. Todd (eds), *Intelligent Philanthropy* (Chicago: University of Chicago Press), pp. 133–48; afterwards published in *Selected Writings. George Herbert Mead*, ed. Andrew Reck (Chicago: University of Chicago Press, 1964; repr. 1981), pp. 392–407.

1930: 'The Philosophies of Royce, James, and Dewey in Their American Setting', *International Journal of Ethics*, 40: 211–31.

1931: 'Dr. A. W. Moore's Philosophy', *University of Chicago Record, New Series*, 17: 47–9.

[1931: Mead dies (26 April)]

1932: *The Philosophy of the Present*, ed. Arthur E. Murphy (La Salle, IL: Open Court; Amherst, NY: Prometheus Books, repr. 2002).

1934: *Mind, Self, and Society*, ed. Charles W. Morris (Chicago: University of Chicago Press; repr. 1997).

1935–6: 'The Philosophy of John Dewey', *International Journal of Ethics*, 46: 64–81.

1936: *Movements of Thought in the Nineteenth Century*, ed. Merritt H. Moore (Chicago: University of Chicago Press; repr. 1972).

1938: *The Philosophy of the Act*, ed. Charles Morris et al. (Chicago: University of Chicago Press).

1964: 'Relative Space–Time and Simultaneity', *Review of Metaphysics*, 17 (ed. David L. Miller): 514–35.

1964: 'Metaphysics', *Review of Metaphysics*, 17 (ed. David L. Miller): 536–56.

1982: *The Individual and the Social Self: Unpublished Work of George Herbert Mead*, ed. David L. Miller (Chicago: University of Chicago Press).

1982: 'Consciousness, Mind, the Self, and Scientific Objects', in *The Individual and the Social Self: Unpublished Work of George Herbert Mead*, ed. David L. Miller (Chicago: University of Chicago Press), pp. 176–96.

1992: 'George Herbert Mead: An Unpublished Essay on Royce and James', *Transactions of the C. H. S. Peirce Society*, 28 (ed. Gary A. Cook): 583–92.

1994: 'George Herbert Mead: An Unpublished Essay Review of Dewey's *Human Nature and Conduct*', *Journal of the History of the Behavioral Sciences*, 30: 374–9.

Anthologies of George Herbert Mead's published writings

1964: *G. H. Mead on Social Psychology*, ed. Anselm Strauss (Chicago: University of Chicago Press).

1964: *Selected Writings. George Herbert Mead*, ed. Andrew Reck (Chicago: University of Chicago Press; repr. 1981).

1968: *George Herbert Mead. Essays on His Social Psychology*, ed. John W. Petras (New York: Teachers College Press).

2001: *Essays on Social Psychology*, ed. Mary Jo Deegan (New Brunswick, NJ: Transaction Publishers).

Secondary

T. Adorno, *Critique of Pure Tolerance* (Boston: Beacon Press, 1965).

J. C. Alexander, 'Cultural Pragmatics: Social Performance Between Ritual and Strategy', *Sociological Theory*, 22 (2004): 527–73.

J. C. Alexander, *Neofunctionalism and After* (Oxford: Blackwell, 1998).

J. C. Alexander, *Twenty Lectures: Sociological Theory after 1945* (New York: Columbia University Press, 1987).

D. Anderson, *Creativity and the Philosophy of C. S. Peirce* (Dordrecht: M. Nijhoff, 1987).

Z. Bauman, *Liquid Modernity* (Cambridge: Polity, 2000).

Z. Bauman, *Modernity and Ambivalence* (Cambridge: Polity, 1991).

U. Beck, A. Giddens and S. Lash, *Reflexive Modernization: Politics, Tradition and Aesthetics in the Modern Social Order* (Cambridge: Polity, 1994).

H. S. Becker, *Outsiders. Studies in the Sociology of Deviance* (New York: The Free Press, 1963).

H. Blumer, 'An Appraisal of Thomas and Znaniecki's "The Polish Peasant in Europe and America"', in *Critiques of Research in the Social Sciences* (New York: Transaction, 1939).

H. Blumer, 'Comment on Lewis' "The Classic American Pragmatists as Forerunners to Symbolic Interactionism"', *Sociological Quarterly*, 18 (1977): 285–9.

H. Blumer, 'George Herbert Mead', in B. Rhea (ed.), *The Future of Sociological Classics* (London: George Allen and Unwin, 1981), pp. 136–69.

H. Blumer, *George Herbert Mead and Human Conduct*, ed. T. J. Morrione (Walnut Creek, CA: Altamira Press, 2004).

H. Blumer, *Industrialization as an Agent of Social Change: A Critical Analysis*, ed. D. Maines and T. Morrione (New York: Aldine de Gruyter, 1990).

H. Blumer, 'Social Psychology', in E. Schmidt (ed.), *Man and Society. A Substantial Introduction to the Social Sciences* (New York: Prentice-Hall, 1937).

H. Blumer, *Symbolic Interactionism. Perspective and Method* (Berkeley: University of California Press, 1969).

H. Blumer, T. Parsons and J. Turner, 'Exchange on Turner, "Parsons as a Symbolic Interactionist"', *Sociological Inquiry*, 45 (1975): 59–68.

P. Bourdieu, *La Distinction. Critique sociale du jugement* (Paris: Minuit, 1979).

D. Bulmer, *The Chicago School of Sociology: Institutionalization, Diversity, and the Rise of Sociology* (Chicago: University of Chicago Press, 1984).

C. Calhoun, *Critical Social Theory* (Oxford: Blackwell, 1995).

H. N. Castle, *Henry Northrup Castle: Letters* (London: Sands, 1902).

R. Collins, *Conflict Sociology: Toward an Explanatory Science* (New York: Academic Press, 1975).

R. Collins, *The Credential Society: An Historical Sociology of Education and Stratification* (New York: Academic Press, 1979).

R. Collins, 'Functional and Conflict Theories of Educational Stratification', *American Sociological Review*, 36 (1971): 1002–19.

R. Collins, *Interaction Ritual Chains* (Princeton, NJ: Princeton University Press, 2004).

R. Collins, 'On the Micro-Foundations of Macro-sociology', *American Journal of Sociology*, 86 (1981): 984–1014.

R. Collins, 'Toward a Neo-Meadian Sociology of Mind', in P. Hamilton (ed.), *George Herbert Mead: Critical Assessments*, 4 vols (London: Routledge, 1992), IV, pp. 263–96.

G. A. Cook, *George Herbert Mead. The Making of a Social Pragmatist* (Urbana, IL: University of Illinois Press, 1993).

L. Coser, 'George Herbert Mead', in *Masters of Sociological Thought: Ideas in Historical and Social Context* (New York: Harcourt Brace Jovanovich, 1971), pp. 333–55.

C. J. Couch, 'Symbolic Interaction and Generic Sociological Principles', *Symbolic Interaction*, 8 (1984): 1–13.

C. J. Couch, *Researching Social Processes in the Laboratory* (Greenwich: JAI Press, 1987).

J. Dewey, 'George Herbert Mead', *Journal of Philosophy*, 28 (1931): 309–14.

J. Dewey, 'Prefatory Remarks', in *Philosophy of the Present*, ed. Arthur E. Murphy (La Salle, IL: Open Court, 1932; Amherst, NY: Prometheus Books, repr. 2002), pp. 31–4.

J. Dewey, *The Public and Its Problems*, in *John Dewey. The Later Works, Volume 2: 1925–1927*, ed. Jo Ann Boydston (Carbondale: Southern Illinois University Press, 1984), pp. 235–372.

J. Dewey, 'The Reflex Arc Concept in Psychology', in *John Dewey. The Early Works, Volume 5: 1889–1892*, ed. Jo Ann Boydston (Carbondale: Southern Illinois University Press, 1972), pp. 84–95.

A. Dodds, J. Lawrence and J. Valsiner, 'The Personal and the Social. Mead's Theory of the "Generalized Other"', *Theory and Psychology*, 7 (1997): 483–503.

J. M. Domingues, *Social Creativity, Collective Subjectivity and Contemporary Modernity* (Basingstoke: Macmillan, 2000).

E. Durkheim, *Pragmatisme et Sociologie* (Paris: Vrin, 1955).

S. N. Eisenstadt, 'Multiple Modernities', in S. N. Eisenstadt (ed.), *Multiple Modernities* (London: Transaction Publishers, 2002), pp. 1–29.

R. E. Faris, *Chicago Sociology, 1920–32* (San Francisco: Chandler Publishing Company, 1967).

A. Feffer, *The Chicago Pragmatists and American Progressivism* (Ithaca: Cornell University Press, 1993).

G. A. Fine, 'The Sad Demise, Mysterious Disappearance, and Glorious Triumph of Symbolic Interactionism', *Annual Review of Sociology*, 19 (1993): 61–87.

B. Fisher and A. Strauss, 'Interactionism', in T. Bottomore and R. Nisbet (eds), *A History of Sociological Analysis* (New York: Oxford University Press, 1978).

A. Gehlen, *Man: His Nature and Place in the World* (New York: Columbia University Press, 1988).

A. Giddens, *The Consequences of Modernity* (Cambridge: Polity, 1990).

A. Giddens, *The Constitution of Society* (Cambridge: Polity, 1984).

A. Gillespie, 'G. H. Mead: Theorist of the Social Act', *Journal for the Theory of Social Behaviour*, 35 (2005): 19–39.

E. Goffman, *The Presentation of the Self in Everyday Life* (New York: Anchor Books, 1959).

J. Habermas, *Between Facts and Norms. Contributions to a Discourse Theory of Law and Democracy* (Cambridge: Polity, 1996).

J. Habermas, 'A Philosophico-Political Profile', *New Left Review*, 151 (1985): 75–105.

J. Habermas, *Postmetaphysical Thinking: Philosophical Essays* (Cambridge: Polity, 1988).

J. Habermas, 'Postscript. Some Concluding Remarks', in M. Aboulafia, M. Brookman and C. Kemp (eds), *Habermas and Pragmatism* (London: Routledge, 2002), pp. 223–33.

J. Habermas, *The Theory of Communicative Action. Volume 2: Lifeworld and System: A Critique of Functionalist Reason* (Cambridge: Polity, 1985).

R. Hardin, *Indeterminacy and Society* (Princeton, NJ: Princeton University Press, 2003).

C. Hartshorne, *Creativity in American Philosophy* (Albany, NY: SUNY Press, 1984).

R. Hinkle, *Founding Theory of American Sociology 1881–1915* (London: Routledge & Kegan Paul, 1980).

G. Hinkle, 'Habermas, Mead, and Rationality', *Symbolic Interaction*, 15 (1992): 315–31.

A. Honneth, *The Fragmented World of the Social. Essays in Social and Political Philosophy* (New York: SUNY Press, 1995).

A. Honneth, *Struggles for Recognition. The Moral Grammar of Social Conflicts* (Cambridge, MA: MIT Press, 1996).

A. Honneth and H. Joas, *Social Action and Human Nature* (Cambridge: Cambridge University Press, 1988).

M. Horkheimer, 'Traditional and Critical Theory', in P. Connerton (ed.), *Critical Sociology* (New York: Penguin, 1976), pp. 206–24.

W. James, *The Principles of Psychology*, vol. 1 (New York: Henry Holt, 1890).

H. Joas, *The Creativity of Action* (Cambridge: Polity, 1996).

H. Joas, 'The Democratization of Differentiation: On the Creativity of Collective Action', in J. C. Alexander and P. Stompka (eds), *Rethinking Progress* (Boston: Unwin, 1990).

H. Joas, 'Durkheim et le pragmatisme. La Psychologie de la conscience et la constitution sociale des catégories', *Revue Française de Sociologie*, 25 (1984): 560–81.

H. Joas, *G. H. Mead. A Contemporary Re-examination of His Thought* (Cambridge, MA: MIT Press, 1985, repr. 1997).

H. Joas, *Pragmatism and Social Theory* (Chicago: University of Chicago Press, 1993).

H. Joas, 'Symbolic Interactionism', in A. Giddens and J. Turner (eds), *Social Theory Today* (Cambridge: Polity, 1987).

H. Joas, *War and Modernity* (Cambridge: Polity, 2003).

M. Kuhn, 'Major Trends in Symbolic Interaction Theory in the Past Twenty-Five Years', *The Sociological Quarterly*, 5 (1964): 61–84.

M. Kuhn and T. S. McPartland, 'An Empirical Investigation of Self-Attitudes', *American Sociological Review*, 19 (1954): 68–75.

D. N. Levine, 'The Idea of the University, Take One: On the Genius of this Place', paper read at the 'Idea of the University Colloquium', University of Chicago, 8 November 2000, pp. 1–15.

D. N. Levine, *Visions of the Sociological Tradition* (Chicago: Chicago University Press, 1995).

J. D. Lewis and R. Smith, *American Sociology and Pragmatism: Mead, Chicago Sociology, and Symbolic Interaction* (Chicago: University of Chicago Press, 1980).

J.-F. Lyotard, *La Condition Postmoderne* (Paris: Minuit, 1979).

M. Maffesoli, *Le Temps des tribus. Le Déclin de l'individualisme dans les sociétés de masse* (Paris: Méridiens Klincksieck, 1988).

D. R. Maines, 'Social Organization and Social Structure in Symbolic Interactionist Thought', *Annual Review of Sociology*, 3 (1977): 235–59.

M. Mann, *The Sources of Social Power. Vol. 2: The Rise of Classes and Nation-States, 1760–1914* (Cambridge: Cambridge University Press, 1993).

K. Mannheim, *Ideology and Utopia: An Introduction to the Sociology of Knowledge* (London: Routledge, 1972).

H. Marcuse, *Reason and Revolution: Hegel and the Rise of Social Theory* (London: Routledge, 1941; repr. 1973).

P. Markell, 'The Potential and the Actual: Mead, Honneth, and the "I" ', in B. Brink and D. Owen (eds), *Recognition and Power. Axel Honneth and the Tradition of Critical Social Theory* (Cambridge: Cambridge University Press, 2006), pp. 100–34.

T. H. Marshall, *Class, Citizenship, and Social Development* (Garden City, NY: Doubleday, 1964).

A. Melucci, *The Playing Self. Person and Meaning in the Planetary Society* (Cambridge: Cambridge University Press, 1996).

L. Menand, *The Metaphysical Club: A Story of Ideas in America* (New York: Farrar, Straus, and Giroux, 2001).

D. L. Miller, *George Herbert Mead. Self, Language and the World* (Chicago: University of Chicago Press, 1973).

T. Parsons, *The Social System* (Glencoe, IL: Free Press, 1951).

T. Parsons, *The Structure of Social Action*, vols I–II (New York: Free Press, 1937; repr. 1968).

R. Perinbanayagam, *Signifying Acts: Structure and Meaning in Everyday Life* (Carbondale, IL: Southern Illinois University Press, 1985).

K.-S. Rehberg, 'Arnold Gehlen's Elementary Anthropology – An Introduction', in *Man: His Nature and Place in the World* (New York: Columbia University Press, 1988), pp. ix–xxxvi.

D. Shalin, 'G. H. Mead, Socialism, and the Progressive Agenda', *American Journal of Sociology*, 93 (1988): 913–51.

D. Shalin, 'Pragmatism and Social Interactionism', *American Sociological Review*, 51 (1986): 9–29.

F. C. Silva, 'G. H. Mead in the History of Sociological Ideas', *Journal of the History of Behavioral Sciences*, 42 (2006): 19–39.

F. C. Silva, *In Dialogue with Modern Times. The Social and Political Thought of G. H. Mead* (Lanham, MD: Lexington Books, forthcoming).

F. C. Silva, 'Re-examining Mead: G. H. Mead on the "Material Reproduction of Society"', *Journal of Classical Sociology*, 7 (2007) (forthcoming).

Q. Skinner, 'A Reply to my Critics', in J. Tully (ed.), *Meaning and Context* (Cambridge: Polity, 1988), pp. 231–88.

A. Strauss, *Negotiations: Varieties, Contexts, Processes, and Social Order* (San Francisco: Jossey-Bass Publishers, 1978).

H. Thayer, *Meaning and Action: A Critical History of Pragmatism* (Indianapolis: Bobbs-Merrill Company, 1968).

G. Therborn, 'Entangled Modernities', *European Journal of Social Theory*, 6 (2003): 293–305.

C. Tucker, 'Herbert Blumer: A Pilgrimage with Pragmatism', *Symbolic Interaction*, 11 (1988): 99–124.

P. Wagner, *A Sociology of Modernity. Liberty and Discipline* (London: Routledge, 1994).

P. Wiener, 'Pragmatism', in P. Wiener (ed.), *Dictionary of the History of Ideas*, 5 vols (New York: Charles Scribner's Sons, 1973), IV, pp. 551–70.

Index